THE X FILES™

Prima's Official Strategy Guide

RICK BARBA

Project Editor: Brooke N. Raymond
Product Manager: Jennifer Crotteau

© 1999 Twentieth Century Fox Film Corporation.

ISBN: 7615-2595-5
Library of Congress Catalog Card Number: 99-67117
Printed in the United States of America

99 00 01 02 GG 10 9 8 7 6 5 4 3 2 1

Table of Contents

PRIMA GAMES

A DIVISION OF PRIMA COMMUNICATIONS, INC.

3875 ATHERTON ROAD
ROCKLIN, CA 95765
(916) 632-4400
WWW.PRIMAGAMES.COM

INTRODUCTION

Welcome to the official strategy guide for one of the most eagerly awaited graphic adventure games of the year. *The X-Files*, one of the great television success stories of the '90s, has a loyal audience whose Internet-based fanaticism is legendary. The show's spectacular success is built on the usual foundation of a good series—compelling stories, fine acting, star power (courtesy of David Duchovny and Gillian Anderson), plus an overarching vision (X-philes call it the show's "mythology") that pulls it all together.

As a game, *The X-Files* brings something original and irresistible to a familiar genre. It combines first-rate storytelling with the distinctive look and feel of the series, courtesy of the show's production company, Ten Thirteen Productions. Then it melds seamless gameplay with "puzzles" that make contextual sense and propel the story forward rather than toss obstacles in its path. Of course, it's still a game. And that's where we come in.

Deep Throat's dying words may have been "Trust no one," but the truth is out there. With the help of the game's creators at Fox Interactive and HyperBole Studios, we've unearthed that truth and packaged it right here for you.

How to Use This Book

This book is so easy to use it's almost embarrassing to explain how. Note, however, that it's no substitute for *The X-Files* game manual. As a "strategy guide," this book assumes you've read all the game's documentation and you're familiar with *The X-Files* game interface for the PlayStation® game console. It is also assumed that you are playing with Artificial Intuition turned off. This strategy guide is divided into two main parts.

THE X-FILES QUICK REFERENCE

The "Quick Reference" section is an alphabetized list of the game's interesting items and major characters. Our advice: *Don't read this section first!* Instead, refer to it when you find unusual items in the game, items that seem to have no significance in terms of actual gameplay. Hard-core X-philes may find little here that they don't already know. But casual fans of the show will get a peek at some of the game's in-jokes and visual references to episodes of the television series.

WALKTHROUGH

This part, as you may have guessed, is a detailed, step-by-step solution path through the game. Hundreds of screenshots visually guide you through every significant event in this very cinematic game. The walkthrough is divided into seven sections, one for each game day. While you play through the game, refer to the contents section to find the day and location at which your investigation is stalled; then turn to that page to get all the answers you seek.

The X-Files: A Quick Reference

If you're not a fanatic watcher of all things *X-Files*, you may miss some of the sly references, in-jokes, and deeper connections to *The X-Files* mythology that punctuate this game. The following handy reference guide lists in alphabetical order some of the game items and characters that refer to elements of the television series and/or *The X-Files* universe.

Note that this guide is by no means comprehensive. For more expanded sources of information on *The X-Files* and related phenomena, see the bibliography at the back of this guide.

3X99

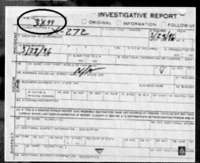

This case file number in Agent Mulder's briefcase (found in his Comity Inn room) is the actual "episode designation" for *The X-Files* game, according to Ten Thirteen Productions.

1013

A special *X-Files* number that appears occasionally on the show. Chris Carter's production company, Ten Thirteen Productions, is named after his birthday, October 13. Note that 10/13 is the birthday of Special Agent Fox Mulder, also.

1121

This Fante County rural route address appears in a number of televised episodes of *The X-Files*, including Scully's digital clock readout (11:21 p.m.) near the end of the show's pilot episode. It refers to the birthday (November 21) of Chris Carter's wife, Dori.

Astadourian, Mary

The name of Agent Willmore's Seattle Police Department partner is also that of the resident researcher/office manager for Ten Thirteen Productions (and Chris Carter's executive assistant) Mary Astadourian. Dedicated X-philes may also remember the Astadourian Lightning Observatory from the "D. P. O." episode (3X03).

Author Rejection

Agent Willmore's rejection notice from *Last Call* (on the futon in his apartment living room) is an oblique reference to the Cigarette-Smoking Man, who in "Musings of a Cigarette-Smoking Man" (4X07) is revealed as a frustrated author with a string of his own literary rejections. Note also that you can read the entire neo-Hemingway story, "Hum of the Earth," actually written by the game's co-designer and music director, Paul Hiaumet.

Byers, John

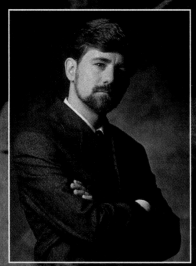

One of the three Lone Gunmen. (See also "Lone Gunmen.") The clean-cut, earnest, professorial John Byers is an information systems genius; with his partner Langly, he can hack into many of the world's most sensitive computer systems. His first appearance, in the "E.B.E." episode (1X16), prompted one of our all-time favorite *X-Files* exchanges: Byers proclaims to Mulder, "Vladimir Zhirinovsky, the leader of the Russian Social Democrats, is being put into power by the most heinous and evil force in the twentieth century." Mulder's response: "Barney?"

Chinese Tiles

The odd tiles found on Wong's person and in his boat hearken back to the macabre Chinese lottery game played in the "Hell Money" episode (3X19). Each tile symbol represents one of the five Chinese elements. Each element, in turn, represents a body part.

In the tile game (created for *The X-Files* by the show's props department), desperate men try to draw a winning tile. If they fail and draw an element tile, they must surrender the corresponding body part. In the "Hell Money" episode, a corrupt doctor manipulates the game to gain organ donors.

Cigarette-Smoking Man

What's his real name? We learned in "Two Fathers" (6X11) that his name may or may not be C.G.B. Spender. He also may or may not have been the assassin who killed JFK and Martin Luther King, Jr.; may or may not have put in the fix on the Buffalo Bills' Super Bowl appearances; may or may not have a long-standing, weighted relationship with Fox Mulder's mother.

Civil War

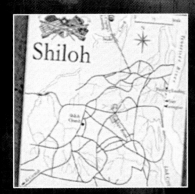

Even a cursory exploration of Agent Willmore's office or apartment reveals his obvious fascination with the Civil War. This mirrors Mulder's experience in "The Field Where I Died" (4X05), one of the show's most powerful episodes. In that show, Mulder meets a woman, Melissa Riedel, who claims their souls were deeply connected in previous lives, including a life in which Mulder was Confederate soldier Sullivan Biddle.

Comity

The name of this Everett inn in the game was also the name of the Caryl County town featured in the "Syzygy" episode (3X13).

"Eat the Corn"

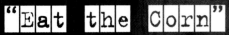

Here's an inside joke. The graffiti on the exterior wall of the dockside Warehouse (facing the boat dock in back) is a reference to an off-color remark once overheard by Gillian Anderson. Apparently, a grip in *The X-Files* Vancouver crew suggested that one of his colleagues "eat the corn" from a substance excreted regularly by most mammals. Anderson found the remark darkly amusing, and is reported to have repeated it on occasion. For one episode—can you find it?—she even spray-painted the phrase (minus the scatological part) on a wall during decoration of a set that required graffiti.

Fairfield Zoo

A brochure in the Comity Inn directs you to the fun-filled Fairfield Zoo, featured in the "Fearful Symmetry" episode (2X18). The zoo was the site of animal abductions near a noted UFO hot spot. (See also "Sophie the Gorilla.")

Frog

This item, found in Wong's boat cabin, is reminiscent of the frog that crawls out of the corpse's chest in *The X-Files* "Hell Money" episode (3X19).

Frohike, Melvin

One of the three Lone Gunmen. (See also "Lone Gunmen.") Melvin Frohike is a photographic expert with a remarkable knowledge of special operations. Of course, he's best known for his lust for Agent Scully. Note in the game that when Agent Willmore learns the Lone Gunmen are Scully's friends, Frohike leans in and adds, "Some of us are more than just friends."

Hell Money

This particular currency, found on James Wong's boat in the game, was featured in the "Hell Money" episode (3X19), where it was used to pay off spirits during the Festival of the Hungry Ghosts. This is based on actual Chinese tradition. During the Chinese New Year and on anniversaries of a relative's death, "hell money" is burned as a gift to the spirit world. (See also "Chinese Tiles.")

Heuvelmans Lake

Did you take a closer look at the coffee mugs on Willmore's and Cook's desks at the FBI Field Office? They're souvenirs from Heuvelmans Lake, home of Big Blue the Southern Serpent in the "Quagmire" episode (3X22). Writer Kim Newton named the lake after Van Heuvels, the Dutch monster researcher whose book *In the Wake of the Sea Serpents* is considered the definitive text on lake monster sightings.

Jose Chung's *From Outer Space*

FROM OUTER SPACE

Jose Chung

X-philes will recognize this book from the third-season episode of the same name (3X20). An author, Jose Chung (played by Charles Nelson Reilly), writes a nonfiction science fiction book about alien abductions starring FBI special agents "Diana Lesky" and "Reynard Muldrake" (described as "a ticking time bomb of insanity"). (Note that reynard is the French word for "fox.")

JFK's Brain

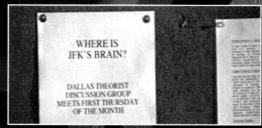

The flyer posted on the bulletin board at the King County Crime Lab refers to the mysterious (and actual) disappearance of assassinated U.S. President John F. Kennedy's brain following his autopsy. Conspiracy theorists (such as the Lone Gunmen) speculate that a forensic examination of JFK's brain tissue would definitively prove the president was shot from the right-front—the infamous "Grassy Knoll" area—rather than from behind, where "patsy" Lee Harvey Oswald is alleged to have fired from the Texas School Depository building.

Keystone Kops

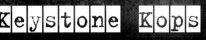

If you click on any TV in the game, you'll see a wild clip of a Keystone Kops movie. This hearkens back to the "Syzygy" episode (3X13), in which Mulder and Scully's hotel room TVs mysteriously show the same Keystone Kops movie on every channel.

Langly, Ringo

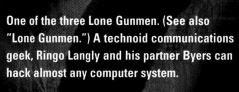

One of the three Lone Gunmen. (See also "Lone Gunmen.") A technoid communications geek, Ringo Langly and his partner Byers can hack almost any computer system.

Lone Gunmen

Frohike, Byers, and Langly (left to right) first appeared in the "E.B.E." episode (1X16). These three conspiracy theorists are paranoid, somewhat manic, and yet right on the mark with many of their revelations (published in their newsletter, *The Magic Bullet*) about secret government sources. Their group name comes from the much-ridiculed "lone gunman theory," the Warren Commission's conclusion that Lee Harvey Oswald acted alone in killing President John F. Kennedy.

The Magic Bullet

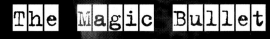

You find a highly entertaining issue of this newsletter, published by the Lone Gunmen, in Agent Mulder's room at the Comity Inn. The title refers to a single bullet reported by the Warren Commission to have passed through President John F. Kennedy's throat and Texas Governor John Connally's torso, finally embedding in Connally's wrist bone—and then found almost completely intact on the governor's stretcher upon his arrival at Parkland Hospital. This bizarre hypothesis is the only way the commission could make their lone-gunman-three-shots theory hold water. Thus, conspiracy theorists have fondly dubbed it the "magic bullet."

Majestic

The name of the game's mysterious shipping company echoes the name of the legendary "Majestic 12" papers allegedly compiled for the Truman administration after the supposed crash in 1947 of a UFO in Roswell, New Mexico. These papers are said to document the existence of a secret government organization whose mission is to conceal all evidence of contact with extraterrestrial life. The Lone Gunmen's newsletter *The Magic Bullet* describes Majestic as "the project control group responsible for security and intelligence and disinformation concerning alien presence here, answerable only to the president."

Morley Cigarettes

The brand of cigarette favored by the Cigarette-Smoking Man, played by actor William B. Davis. (See "Cigarette-Smoking Man.")

MUFON

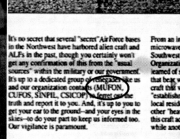

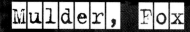

Mentioned in *The Magic Bullet* newsletter, MUFON is the acronym for Mutual UFO Network, a support group of alien abductees who first appear in the "Nisei" episode (3X09) and reappear prominently in the dramatic "Memento Mori" episode (4X15).

Mulder, Fox

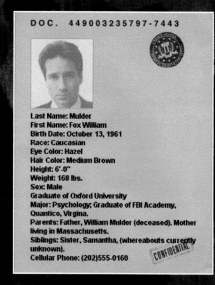

Last Name: Mulder
First Name: Fox William
Birth Date: October 13, 1961
Race: Caucasian
Eye Color: Hazel
Hair Color: Medium Brown
Height: 6'-0"
Weight: 168 lbs.
Sex: Male
Graduate of Oxford University
Major: Psychology; Graduate of FBI Academy, Quantico, Virgina.
Parents: Father, William Mulder (deceased). Mother living in Massachusetts.
Siblings: Sister, Samantha, (whereabouts currently unknown).
Cellular Phone: (202)555-0160

DOC. 449003235797-7443

Anyone even remotely familiar with *The X-Files* phenomenon knows Fox William Mulder. This file from his FBI dossier provides basic background information. His sister Samantha's mysterious abduction at age 8 has been a driving force behind his obsession with the X-Files section of the FBI. Other Mulder profile items:

Badge Number: JTT047101111
Height: 6 Feet
Rank: Special Agent
Marital Status: Unmarried
Distinguishing Marks/Features: Mole on right cheek

Pendrell, Sean

Named for a street in Vancouver, Agent Sean Pendrell is the hardworking investigator at the FBI Sci-Crime Lab who nurtures a crush on Agent Scully. (Doesn't everybody?) Played in the series by actor Brendan Beiser, Agent Pendrell was introduced in the "Nisei" episode (3X09) and appears in many third- and fourth-season episodes of *The X-Files*. Unfortunately, poor Pendrell takes a fatal bullet in the "Tempus Fugit" episode (4X17).

Ramones Posters

Yes, Agent Willmore is a Ramones fan. True fans of *The X-Files* know that Lone Gunman Langly often wears Ramones T-shirts and is a huge fan of the band.

Scully, Dana

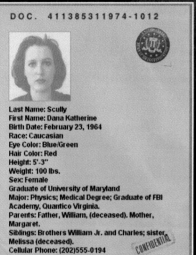

DOC. 411385311974-1012

Last Name: Scully
First Name: Dana Katherine
Birth Date: February 23, 1964
Race: Caucasian
Eye Color: Blue/Green
Hair Color: Red
Height: 5'-3"
Weight: 100 lbs.
Sex: Female
Graduate of University of Maryland
Major: Physics; Medical Degree; Graduate of FBI Academy, Quantico Virginia.
Parents: Father, William, (deceased). Mother, Margaret.
Siblings: Brothers William Jr. and Charles; sister, Melissa (deceased).
Cellular Phone: (202)555-0194
CONFIDENTIAL

If you don't know who Dana Katherine Scully is, you're playing the wrong game, my friend. Her confidential FBI dossier gives you the basics, but let us add a bit of Scully trivia: She called her father, a navy captain, "Ahab." His nickname for her— "Starbuck." (If you don't recognize those names, you might want to check out Herman Melville's *Moby Dick*.)
Other Scully profile items:
Badge Number: 2317-616
Height: 5' 3"
Rank: Special Agent
Marital Status: Unmarried
Distinguishing Marks/Features: Tattoo on lower back
Senior Thesis: "Einstein's Twin Paradox: A New Interpretation"
Medical Residency: Forensic pathology

Severed Hand

Did you find the severed hand in the King County Medical Examiner's Office? (It's in a jar on a shelf behind the autopsy table.) This scintillating sight recalls the "Tempus Fugit" and "Max" episodes (4X17/18) chronicling the crash of Flight 549, an airliner carrying 134 people, including famous UFO abductee Max Fenig. The Fox Network's Standards and Practices Department excised a brief shot of a severed hand from the crash-site footage. Could this be the same hand? Or has the original hand gone the way of JFK's brain? *Why is there such a conspiracy of silence about the hand?*

Skinner, Walter S.

FBI Assistant Director Walter S. Skinner was Fox Mulder and Dana Scully's immediate supervisor until "The Beginning" (6X01). A tough, no-nonsense ex-Marine, he's developed a reluctant fondness for the unorthodox pair of agents working the X-Files section. Although no longer their boss, Skinner often finds himself caught in the middle between Mulder and Scully's investigations and the dark, powerful operatives (Cigarette-Smoking Man foremost among them) seeking to undermine those investigations.

Sophie the Gorilla

Sophie the Gorilla
Lived!

This famed Fairfield Zoo primate used American Sign Language in the "Fearful Symmetry" episode (2X18) to communicate key information about UFO animal abductions. (See also "Fairfield Zoo.")

Stiletto

This type of alien blade makes its first *X-Files* appearance in the hands of the deadly alien bounty hunter in the two-part "Colony/End Game" episode (2X16/17). (During the second part, a clone of Mulder's sister Samantha reveals that the only way to kill the alien is to pierce the base of its skull.) The stiletto reappears in the final episode of the third season, "Talitha Cumi" (3X24). Mulder discovers it in a lamp where his mother concealed it.

Sunflower Seeds

Did you notice the ashtray full of seed shells in Agent Mulder's Comity Inn room? Sunflower seeds are Mulder's snack of preference. He first discusses inheriting his father's taste for the seeds in the "Aubrey" episode (2X12). He also talks in his sleep about wanting sunflower seeds in the dramatic opening episode of the third season, "The Blessing Way" (3X01).

Sweet Potato Pie

Did you check out this flyer for the Everett Diner in the alcove of Mulder's room at the Comity Inn? The ad for the diner's "world-famous sweet potato pie" brings back stomach-clenching memories of Agent Mulder wolfing down piece after piece of that same type of pie in a diner in "Jose Chung's *From Outer Space*" (3X20). Note also that if you dial the Everett Diner's phone number—1-360-555-0177—you get a recorded message touting the pie: "You can't eat just one piece!"

Vodka and Orange Juice Concentrate

Agent Mulder was first seen sipping this somewhat pathetic concoction—orange juice concentrate spooned into a vodka bottle—while killing time in another Comity motel room in the "Syzygy" episode (3X13).

Willmore, Craig

Does the name Craig Willmore sound familiar? If you're a truly rabid X-phile, you remember it from the "Syzygy" episode (3X13). The two "aligned" high school girls, Terri and Margi, discuss a boy they dislike in the school gym. His name: Craig Willmore. *Hate him, hate him, wouldn't want to date him.* Are you listening, Detective Astadourian?

INTELLIGENCE NETWORK GATEWAY

Name:	Willmore, Craig
DOB:	10-19-63
Height: 6'-1"	Sex: male
Weight: 175 lbs.	Race: caucasian
Hair:	brown
Eyes:	hazel

ING
PHOTO
E-MAIL
APB
QUIT

Field Notes
Graduated from Northwestern University with B.A. in History
Minor: Criminology
Graduated from New York University with M.A.

Clear

Wong, James

The game's tumor-riddled Chinese fisherman happens to share his name with one of the original series writers and co-executive producers. The real James Wong co-wrote (with partner Glen Morgan) such memorable *X-Files* episodes as "Squeeze" (1X02, introducing the memorable Eugene Victor Tooms); "Ice" (1X07); "E.B.E." (1X16, introducing the Lone Gunmen); "Tooms" (1X20, introducing Assistant Director Skinner); "Little Green Men" (2X01), and "Die Hand Die Verletzt" (2X14).

X

Played by Steven Williams, X is the shadowy high-level government source whose tense, edgy baritone subtly guides and manipulates agents Mulder and Scully in their pursuit of the truth. X makes his first *The X-Files* appearance—in "The Host" (2X02)—with an anonymous phone call to Agent Mulder. His message: "You have a friend in the FBI." But is he a friend, or is he in league with dark powers? As always, the truth is far more complicated than simple categories can convey.

Yoga with David

Another inside joke. This flyer is posted on the bulletin board in the meeting room of the FBI Seattle Office. HyperBole's Greg Roach, who designed the game and directed the live-action sequences, reports that David Duchovny is a yoga enthusiast, so the production team provided a yoga instructor for him for the duration of the shoot in Seattle.

Walkthrough Introduction

Welcome to the official walkthrough for the game millions of PlayStation gamers have craved since *The X-Files* first wriggled its way into our paranoid hearts like so many oily black worms. Yes, the truth is out there. But it's also in *here*. Trust no one … except us.

You, the player, guide the actions of Craig Willmore, a special agent of the FBI based in the bureau's Seattle Field Office. You could think of Willmore as a host and yourself as the alien entity who controls him. (If he gets out of hand … *get the alien stiletto ready*.)

The walkthrough uses these simple abbreviations:

F   Forward
L   Left
R   Right
U   Up
D   Down

A Note About "UberVariables"

One of the coolest things about HyperBole's powerful VirtualCinema game engine is its ability to monitor psychological variables. This makes for great replayability. Yes, attitudes count in *The X-Files*. Agent Willmore's demeanor toward certain characters in the game—in particular, Detective Mary Astadourian and Agent Mark Cook—affects their direct responses and later attitudes toward Willmore.

But that's not all. Willmore's own psychological state unfolds according to choices you make. His paranoia, his sense of loss, and his propensity to "believe" evolve from decisions you make in the game. The game engine tags these psychological tracking choices with the term "UberVariables."

UBERVARIABLE 1: PARANOIA

If your version of Agent Willmore follows the ultimate X-Maxim, "Trust No One," you may see some pretty spooky things in the course of your investigation—twitching corpses, shadowy followers, and the like.

UBERVARIABLE 2: LOSS

Agent Willmore is a divorced father in *The X-Files*. Does your Willmore spend time gazing at the bittersweet remnants of his marriage and fatherhood? If so, the notes and messages from his ex-wife Barbara soften significantly in tone. If, on the other hand, you choose indifferent responses to other characters, Willmore's psyche (and past) hardens somewhat.

UBERVARIABLE 3: "THE X-TRACK"

Is your Willmore a Mulder-esque "True Believer" or is he more of a Scully-like skeptic? Your willingness to believe in the paranormal will enhance some of the choices and explanations available to Agent Willmore during the game.

Review Your Field Notes

Site: Comity Inn
Interview desk clerk abt. 2 FBI agents:
Fox Mulder/Dana Scully – Nothing unusual
abt. agts. "Checked in, left that eve..."

Search rooms: Agt. Mulder's – sunflower
seeds, paperback book, copy of
newsletter "Magic Bullet," briefcase.
Mulder had been drinking.

Note: Pass-through door betw. rooms
locked. Opened by clerk.

Notepad   Navigation   E-mail   OFF

The X-Files provides an excellent way for you to deepen your understanding of events and other characters in the game. Access your PDA (Personal Digital Assistant) from inventory and select the Pencil icon to regularly review Agent Willmore's field notes. These notes provide a thorough record of your activities; in some cases, they may offer clarification of certain aspects of your investigation. A good tactic: Read them after you visit each location.

THE TRUTH IS OUT THERE

Game Opening

SEATTLE, WASHINGTON

A rat sniffs a Morley brand cigarette butt among some old crates near a dock. Nearby, two FBI special agents—Fox Mulder and Dana Scully—approach a dilapidated warehouse. Mulder picks the door lock, enters with Scully, and discovers an odd black powder on the floor.

Suddenly, three gunmen, weapons blazing, burst through the doorway. Scully takes a shoulder hit and Mulder drags her to cover. Then a brilliant light radiates from above. We hear the gunmen's agonized screams.

The light fades. After a beat, Mulder pops up from behind a crate, his gun drawn. Nothing moves. He squints into the darkness at something unsettling.

WELCOME TO
ANOTHER CLASSIC *X-FILES* MOMENT.

Day1, April 2, 1996

FBI Field Office, Seattle, 9:14 a.m.

HALLWAY

Paranoid

1 The game begins with Agent Craig Willmore's arrival at the FBI Seattle Field Office just four days after Mulder and Scully's disappearance. Here's the layout of the office

2 Agent Willmore runs into his office mate and fellow agent, Mark Cook. Select any Emotion icon to respond to Agent Cook.

3 After Cook returns to his office, go F, L to face Willmore's office. Move the pointer over the desk chair. When the pointer becomes the Action Hand, click to sit at Willmore's desk.

NOTE

Remember, Willmore's attitude can affect the psychological "track" he follows in the game. For example, if you select Indifferent here, a letter from Willmore's ex-wife will be on his office desk. If you select Paranoid, of course, you send Willmore down the creepy Paranoia track.

WILLMORE'S OFFICE

4 Answer the phone, will you? Director Shanks wants Willmore to come to his office.

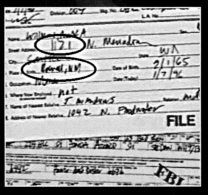

FILE

FBI

5 Pick up Willmore's case files from the desktop and examine them. Note the street address and place of birth of the suspect, Mark A. Williams. (See "1121" "*The X-Files* Quick Reference.")

THE X FILES

Day1, April 2, 1996

NOTE

If your game-opening response in the hallway was Indifferent to Cook, a letter from Willmore's ex-wife Barbara sits on the desktop. Read it to get a peek into Willmore's psyche.

6 Look D to see the desk drawer. Open the drawer and get Willmore's important law enforcement items—Badge, Handcuffs, and Gun.

7 Look up to close the drawer, and then go 2F, R, F, L, F to step into the FBI Meeting Room.

MEETING ROOM

8 Turn L and click on the cabinet at left marked "Authorized Agents Only." Take the items—Binoculars, Lockpick, Camera, Flashlight, Nightvision goggles, and Evidence kit.

9 Go R, F, then exit through the meeting room door (using the door knob) to reach Director Shanks's office door. Go F again to enter Shanks's office.

SHANKS'S OFFICE

Shanks introduces you to Assistant Director Walter Skinner, who describes the priority case—two missing FBI agents. He hands you a Folder with background information and Photos of Mulder and Scully.

Talk to Skinner and ask all questions. In particular, ask what case Mulder and Scully were working on. Skinner gives you their travel requisition form.

> **TALK** HISTORY
> Are they romantically involved?
> Where were they last seen? ▼

Examine the travel requisition form to learn Mulder and Scully set up base at the Comity Inn in nearby Everett, Washington.

Talk to Shanks and ask all questions. He tells you to file an APB (All Points Bulletin) and hand off your current assignments to Agent Cook. Go 2L, F to end up in the hallway.

HALLWAY

Select any Emotion icon to respond to Agent Cook. (Our favorite is the Mean response.) Then go 2F across the hallway to Agent Cook's office.

COOK'S OFFICE

Talk to Cook and tell him Shanks wants you to give your cases to him. Press ● to bring up inventory, then select the Case files and click their icon on Cook. He's most grateful. You can ask Cook to put out the APB, too, but it's more fun to do it yourself. Plus, it pushes Willmore further down the distrustful Paranoia track, our favorite.

NOTE

If Willmore received and read the letter from his ex-wife i his office, you can tell Cook about it now.

Exit Cook's office. If you asked Cook to send the APB, Skinner waits for you in the hallway. If you decided to send the APB yourself, return to Willmore's office.

WILLMORE'S OFFICE

17 Sit at the desk and activate the computer.

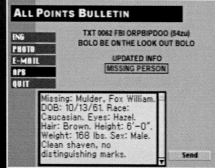

ALL POINTS BULLETIN

	TXT 0062 FBI ORPBIPDOO (54zu)
ING	BOLO BE ON THE LOOK OUT BOLO
PHOTO	
E-MAIL	UPDATED INFO
APB	MISSING PERSON
QUIT	

Missing: Mulder, Fox William.
DOB: 10/13/61. Race:
Caucasian. Eyes: Hazel.
Hair: Brown. Height: 6'-0".
Weight: 168 lbs. Sex: Male.
Clean shaven, no
distinguishing marks.

Send

18 Use the D-pad arrows to select APB—the correct info on Mulder and Scully automatically appears—and then select Send. You can check your e-mail, too, if you want. Nothing important today. When you're finished, select Quit and exit the office.

HALLWAY

19 In the hallway you meet Skinner, who suggests you start your fieldwork at the Comity Inn. This adds the Comity Inn to your PDA as a travel destination.

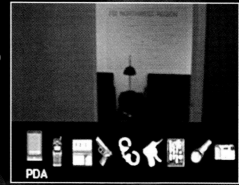

20 Press ● to bring up your inventory. The PDA will be automatically highlighted. Press ✕ to select it.

PDA

21 Use the D-pad arrows to highlight Everett, then press ✕ to select it.

Press ✕ to select the Comity Inn. (See "Comity" in *The X-Files* Quick Reference.")

Day1, April 2, 1996

19

Comity Inn
EVERETT, WASHINGTON

Agent Willmore and Assistant Director Skinner arrive at the Comity Inn in Everett.

COMITY INN: FRONT DESK

Turn left to see the little girl at the gumball machine. To nudge Willmore further down the "Loss" track and soften the edge of his character, talk to the girl's mother and then ask the girl if she'd like a gumball. What a guy!

Select your FBI Badge from inventory and click the Badge icon on the desk clerk. Willmore flashes it to command some authority. (For fun, ring the desk bell a couple of times, too.)

NOTE

The motel desk clerk describes Agent Mulder as "spooky." Inside joke! Serious X-philes know this is the nickname Mulder earned at the Quantico FBI Training Academy.

Talk to the clerk and ask all questions. In particular, get the info on Mulder and Scully's rental car and ask to see their rooms.

MULDER'S ROOM

Look at *The Magic Bullet* newsletter on the desk and read all the paranoia that's fit to print.

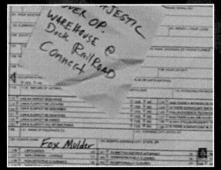

Look at the open briefcase on the bed and examine Mulder's investigative report. Aha! Agent Mulder's report classifies his investigation as an X-File, case number 3X99. Note also the info on the blue sticky note about a "Majestic cover op" and a "railroad connect" to a "warehouse @ dock." Hmmm.

29 Go F toward the front door and then turn left. Look at the nightstand by the bed for a close-up.

30 Pick up the book *From Outer Space* by Jose Chung from the nightstand by the bed. (See "Jose Chung's *From Outer Space*" in "*The X-Files* Quick Reference.")

31 Go F, L, and turn on the TV. Interesting programming! (See "Keystone Kops" in "*The X-Files* Quick Reference.") Move B to turn off the Kops.

32 Look at the vodka bottle atop the TV. (See "Vodka and Orange Juice Concentrate" in "*The X-Files* Quick Reference.")

33 Go F through the door into Scully's room.

SCULLY'S ROOM

34 Go F toward Skinner, then turn L. You see a laptop computer on a desk and an open bible on the nightstand.

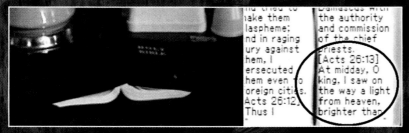

35 Look at the Bible in Scully's room for a close-up, then look again to open the book. Read the marked passages, using the direction pad arrows to turn pages. Note St. Paul's references to "a light from heaven, brighter than the sun," his entreaty to "King Agrippa," and his story of an ill-fated sea voyage.

36 Back up from the Bible close-up. Look at Scully's laptop computer for a close-up, then take the laptop.

Day1, April 2, 1996

21

Turn R and talk to Skinner. Press ● to highlight the Phone icon at the top of the screen, then press ✕ to select it. Willmore suggests checking the motel's log of outgoing calls. Then ask all other questions.

Open the door to the left of Skinner to exit into the parking lot. Go forward through the office door to approach the front desk.

FRONT DESK

#	DATE	DESCRIPTION	AMOUNT
1	3/29/96	ROOM RENTAL/103 /1	$44.00
	3/29/96	ROOM TAX/103 /1	$4.00
	3/29/96	ROOM RENTAL/104 /1	$44.00
	3/29/96	ROOM TAX/104 /1	$4.00

```
***PAID IN ADVANCE........$646.80

          PHONE SERVICES
Washington, DC
202-555-0149  103 /8:24AM    8 min.
Rate $02.12/min      Total Charge $16.96

Seattle, WA
206-555-0182  104 /9:22AM    2 min.
Rate $00.94/min      Total Charge $01.
```

Talk to the clerk. Select the Phone icon again to get a record of outgoing calls by Mulder and Scully. Click on the record for a close-up. Note the two numbers called: 202-555-0149 in Washington, DC, and 206-555-0182 in Seattle.

In inventory, select your cell phone. Enter the Washington, DC, phone number—remember, it's long-distance, so dial "1" first. (Use the D-pad arrows to highlight each number you want, then press ✕ to select the number.)

NOTE

You can try to call the Seattle phone number, too, but you get no answer.

After entering the number, press the call button (with the green phone icon, just under CLEAR) and enjoy Willmore's brief conversation with Frohike. (See "Frohike" in "*The X-Files* Quick Reference.")

Use your PDA to travel back to the FBI Field Office in Seattle.

FBI Field Office

When you arrive, Skinner tells you he'll be reviewing his notes in the meeting room. Go F, L, F into Willmore's office.

WILLMORE'S OFFICE

Note that when Willmore enters his office, he sets Scully's laptop computer on a side table.

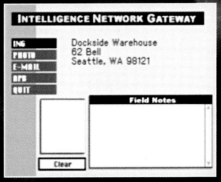

44 Sit at the desk and access Willmore's computer. Select ING (Intelligence Network Gateway). Under Search Category, select the Phone button. Scroll back up to the Search Category entry field to bring up phone numbers. Scroll to the Seattle phone number, 206-555-0182.

45 Scroll down to highlight the Search button and press X to select it. An address appears and a new location (Dockside Warehouse) appears on your PDA travel list for Seattle.

46 Quit your computer and use your PDA to travel to the Dockside Warehouse in Seattle.

Dockside Warehouse
SEATTLE, WASHINGTON

FRONT OF WAREHOUSE

47 Look familiar? Yes, this is the same warehouse you saw in the game's introductory sequence—the place where gunmen attacked Mulder and Scully. Let's find evidence of that event, shall we? Approach Skinner to see the lock on the warehouse door.

Lockpick

NOTE
You can pick the lock on either the front door or the back door of the warehouse.

48 Select your Lockpick from inventory and use it on the warehouse door lock. Open the door.

WAREHOUSE INTERIOR

Inside, you must collect various items by using your FBI Evidence kit. The following steps outline the route to each item.

49 For consistency, each route starts from this spot just inside the front doors of the warehouse.

To Get Blood and Bullet Evidence

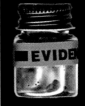

50 From the warehouse front door, go F, R, F, L, F and look down. Look at the bloodstain on the floor for a close-up. In inventory, select your Evidence kit and use it on the bloodstain to collect a sample.

After Willmore reports the blood finding to Skinner, look up and move the pointer over the post at right until it becomes the Eye pointer.

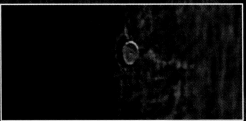

52 Look at the post for a close-up. Move the pointer around the post until you can look again and get a close-up of a bullet embedded in the post.

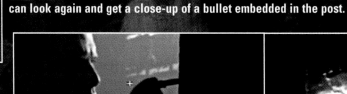

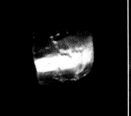

53 Again, use the Evidence kit to extract the bullet.

To Find the Cigarette Butt

54 From the warehouse front door, go 2F, R, 2F, R, and look at the floor (lower left, near the bottom of the screen) to get a closer view of the cigarette butt.

55 Use the Evidence kit to collect the butt. A Morley! Know anybody who smokes that brand?

NOTE

You don't have to find the cigarette butt to successfully complete the game.

From the warehouse door, go 3F, L, 3F to enter the warehouse office. You end up at the foot of a staircase. In inventory, select the Flashlight to activate it. Now your pointer becomes a flashlight beam.

Continue 4F up the stairs to the second floor. Use the toolbox near the bottom of the screen.

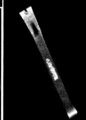

Agent Willmore approaches the toolbox and borrows a crowbar.

Go R, 2F, D, 2F to return to the office and see Skinner, who says, "This phone is DOA." Continue out of the office, going 4F, R, 2F, and then look down at the crates (near the front door). Click on the crates for a close-up.

Use the crowbar to open the crate.

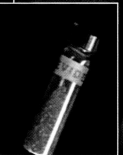

Use the Evidence kit to collect a sample of black powder from the crate. Willmore now leaves the crowbar on the floor. You don't need it anymore.

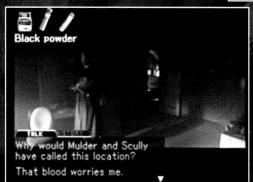

Now that you've collected all evidence, you should report to Skinner on what you've found. Return to the warehouse office and talk to Skinner. Ask all questions and use all Idea icons—Blood, Black powder, Morley butt—on Skinner to get his reactions.

From the spot where you face Skinner, go 7F, R, F, L and open the back door to exit the warehouse. (Alternate path: Exit the front door and go around to the back outside the warehouse.) You step out to see a man washing a boat.

BOAT DOCK (BACK OF WAREHOUSE)

Go L, F, R, F, 2R, F, L to walk down the dock ramp and face the man (James Wong) washing his boat. Use your FBI Badge on Wong.

Talk to Wong and ask all questions. When he tells you about the fish drying up, a Fish stocks icon appears. Select it to ask Wong about Fish stocks.

NOTE

Try offering Wong the Jose Chung book, *From Outer Space.*

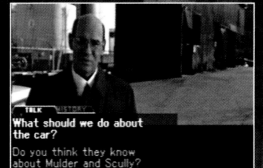

Return to front of the warehouse; go L, F, 2L, U, F, L, 2F, R, F to meet Skinner at the car. He points out a sedan that's been following you. Ask all questions.

Go F once, then *quickly* press ● and select your Camera from inventory. Press ✕ to take a photo of the sedan as it screeches away.

Use your PDA to travel to the Crime Lab in Seattle.

King County Crime Lab
SEATTLE, WASHINGTON

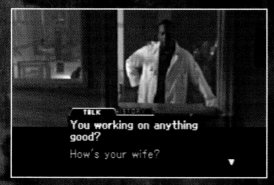

Talk to John Amis and ask all questions.

Select all Evidence icons—Blood, Bullet, Black powder, Morley butt—to give them to Amis for analysis. Industrial-grade lead? Then use your PDA to travel back to the Field Office in Seattle.

FBI Field Office
MEETING ROOM

Go R, F into the meeting room, where Skinner goes through his notes.

Talk to Skinner. Ask all questions and use all idea icons (including the new one, Fisherman) to trigger Skinner's return to Washington, DC. Skinner takes a sample of the warehouse blood to be analyzed at the FBI's Sci-Crime Lab back in Washington, DC. Note his directive to keep the warehouse under surveillance. Then exit the meeting room and go to Willmore's office.

Day1, April 2, 1996

WILLMORE'S OFFICE

72 Sit at Willmore's desk to trigger Cook's entry. (Cook appears only *after* you talk to Skinner in the meeting room.) Talk to Cook using any dialogue path. Cook offers to call the Computer Crime Division to run a check on Scully's laptop. If you agree, he takes the laptop and puts it in the evidence cabinet. If you don't agree, your paranoia forces Willmore to do it himself later.

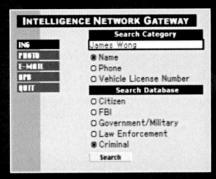

73 Optional: Access Willmore's computer and run a background check on James Wong. Here's how: Select ING, and under Search Database, select Criminal. Highlight the entry field under Search Category and press ✕ to bring up names. Keep pressing ✕ until Wong's name appears.

74 Select Search. And there he is. Not a pretty picture, eh?

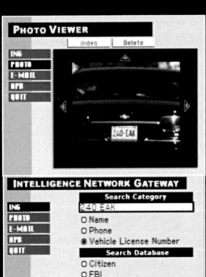

75 You can also run a search on the sedan that followed you to the warehouse. Select PHOTO to bring up the Photo Viewer. If you've snapped more than one photo, use the direction pad arrows to scroll to the photo that shows the sedan's license plate number: 240 EAK.

Select ING and under Search Database, select Government/Military. Under Search Category, select Vehicle License Number. Scroll up to the entry field under Search Category and press ✕ to bring up license numbers. Scroll to the sedan's license, 240 EAK. Select Search.

76 Uh-oh. Restricted data. Skinner fears an underworld connection, but this connection looks to be well above ground.

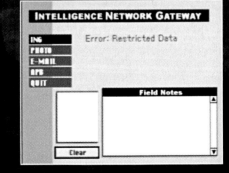

77 Exit the office. If you didn't ask Cook to run the computer check on Scully's laptop, Willmore puts it in the evidence cabinet. Use your PDA to travel back to the Dockside Warehouse in Seattle.

Dockside Warehouse

78 A dark car arrives and some spooky looking fellows carry a crate through the front door of the warehouse. Let's sneak around back and see what they're up to. After the intruders enter the warehouse, go F, R, 2F, L, F, L to the warehouse's back door. (If you wait too long, they return to the car so you can't observe their activities.)

CAUTION

Warning: Don't leave your hiding place until the intruders enter the warehouse and close the door!

79 Pick the lock with your Lockpick, then open the door to enter the warehouse.

80 Go R, F, L, 2F to see the suspicious activity. Select your Binoculars from inventory for a close-up view of the men loading items into their crate from a hidden storage compartment in the floor.

81 Go F, L, F, 2R, and look D to see the bloodstain again. (It might help to use your Flashlight here.) Move the pointer to the left of the blood stain until it becomes the Action Hand. Select that spot to have Agent Willmore open and examine the now-empty compartment.

82 Use your PDA to travel to your apartment in Seattle.

Eavelyn Apartments
SEATTLE, WASHINGTON

Click on the apartment door to enter.

Turn 2L and examine the detritus of Willmore's failures littering the futon sofa.

A quick perusal of his rooms reveals Willmore's abiding interests—the Ramones, the Civil War, and above all, his daughter Elizabeth.

Turn left and follow the hallway to the bedroom.

Check out those wild FBI ties on the dresser and other items in the room.

Get to know Agent Willmore better. Rifle through his journal on the nightstand next to the bed. (It's right under the lamp.) Does Craig have a life beyond the bureau? You decide.

You might want to take a peek out the window before you hit the sack. How paranoid are you?

Select the bed to sleep. Willmore's head hits the pillow like a crate of industrial-grade lead.

THE X FILES

Willmore's Apartment

You start Day 2 in the bedroom of Willmore's home in the Eavelyn Apartments.

After the alarm clock jolts you awake, stagger into the bathroom and take a peek at yourself in the mirror. *What a guy*! Use the PDA to travel to the FBI Field Office.

FBI Field Office

Hey, look. Cook's on the floor. Move the pointer over him and press × to revive the big goof.

Go F, R, F and open the evidence cabinet to discover that Scully's laptop computer is missing. When you hear the phone ring, enter Willmore's office.

WILLMORE'S OFFICE

Sit at the desk and answer the phone. Agent Pendrell reports from the Sci-Crime Lab in Washington, D.C. Bad news: The blood on the warehouse floor is from Agent Scully. Now her laptop is gone, too. Could anything else go wrong? You bet! Cook appears with news of Wong's murder. Maybe you should call it a day.

After Cook appears with the news of Wong's death, ask Cook all questions. Think back. Did you tell your buddy Cook about Wong? Maybe you just forgot. Or not. Use the PDA to travel to the Dockside Warehouse in Seattle.

TALK
How did you know I questioned Wong?
Did you see who hit you?

Dockside Warehouse, Seattle: 9:51 a.m.

BOAT DOCK

Use your FBI Badge on Officer Mendoza to enter the crime scene area.

Talk to the medical examiner (the man on the right). Ask all questions of the droll fellow. He's pretty sure aliens killed JFK. He also suggests you check with Detective Astadourian for more info.

Talk to the photographer (at left). He doesn't know much, but ask all questions anyway. He promises to send copies of his photos.

Go L, F to approach Detective Mary Astadourian of the Seattle Police Department. Talk to her and immediately explain the bureau's interest in the missing FBI agents. She appreciates your candor and will prove a valuable ally in your ongoing investigation.

Look down at Wong's corpse and peruse the objects around it. Note the Morley cigarette butt—same brand as you found in the warehouse. But wait, Wong said he didn't smoke, remember? And what's up with those Chinese tiles? (See "Chinese tiles" in the "Quick Reference" section.)

Ask Astadourian all other questions. Willmore and Astadourian automatically board Wong's boat, the *Agrippa*.

Wong's Boat: The *Agrippa*

MAIN DECK

Astadourian examines the hold, which reveals no container for caught fish. Suspicious, eh? Talk to Astadourian and select both Idea icons (Wong and Fish stocks). Then go F through the cabin door.

CABIN

Go ahead. Examine all the weird, exotic items in the cabin. Most are merely interesting—candles, pandas, dead frogs, and the like—but not pertinent.

THE X FILES

32

Prima's Official Strategy Guide

Look D and click on the stack of bank notes. What the hell kind of money is this?

16 Turn L and select the yellow *Tarakan* slicker. Willmore examines it. (This gives you the Slicker Idea icon later.)

Turn R twice and open the cabinet door. (Move the pointer over the cabinet knob and select it.) Select the drug bottles in the cabinet to examine them. (This gives you the Wong's Drugs Idea icon later.) Go R, F to exit the boat cabin.

MAIN DECK/DOCKSIDE

Turn 2R and talk to Detective Astadourian. Use the two new Idea icons, Slicker and Wong's drugs.

19 After you talk to Astadourian, the medical examiner hauls off Wong's body and the Harbor Master returns with a couple of mugs of good Seattle coffee. Go R, F, R to face the Astadourian and the Harbor Master on the dock.

20 Talk to the Harbor Master. Ask all questions and use all four available Idea icons—Slicker, Warehouse, Wong, Fish stocks. He knows about the *Tarakan*, an ocean-going tug that recently burned at sea, and about its owner, Majestic Shipping. Wait—could this be the same "Majestic" noted by Mulder in his investigative report? Let's go check out the boat.

NOTE

If you're on the Paranoia track, you might see something interesting as the medical examiner rolls Wong down the ramp. Watch the body carefully.

21 Use your PDA. In Seattle, travel to the *Tarakan*.

Camden Impound Dock: The *Tarakan*

22 Listen to the Harbor Master tell the odd story of the *Tarakan*. Willmore notes the unusual burn pattern and wonders how an exterior fire could kill the entire crew. Good question, Craig.

Look U and note the upper deck. Weird! Everything's melted and burned in one spot.

Go L, F, R to face the gangplank.

TARAKAN MAIN DECK

From the bottom of the gangplank on the dock, go F, R, F, and then 2F through the open hatch at right (circled here).

You should see the sign that reads DILARANG MASUK KECUALI CREW. This is the entry to the hold. From here, go R, D to enter the hold.

TARAKAN HOLD

From the bottom of the stairs, go 2F, R, F, and look down to see the crates.

Click on one of the crates for a close-up of the strange black eagle logo.

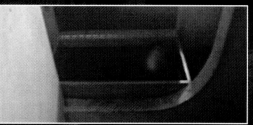

From the crates, turn L and go 3F to see the box. Open the box to discover ... *my God, the Russians are smuggling bowling balls into America*!

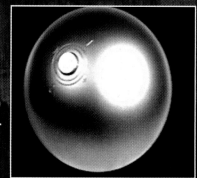

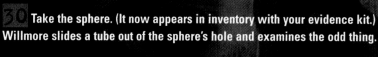 Take the sphere. (It now appears in inventory with your evidence kit.) Willmore slides a tube out of the sphere's hole and examines the odd thing.

From the box, turn L, then go 3F, R, F, L, 2F, U, F, L, F to exit the hold. From the hold doorway, go R, F, L and click on the open passage to see another CREW sign on a door below. Open the door to enter the crew cabin area.

THE X FILES

CREW CABINS (UPPER DECK)

From the bottom of the stairs, go U, 2F to enter the first cabin.

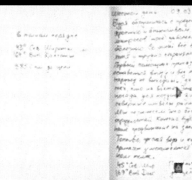

33 Look at the Russian captain's journal on the table to get a close-up, then pick it up and flip pages. It's in Cyrillic, of course. (When you close the journal, it appears in the inventory with your Evidence kit.)

34 Go R, F to exit the first cabin. Go F again to enter the second cabin.

35 Turn R and look D to see the open safe. Click on the safe for a close-up.

36 Take the payroll log from the safe. It, too, is in Cyrillic.

37 Go R, F to exit the second cabin. Go F to the exterior door. Open the exterior door to step out onto the upper deck walkway. Nice view!

UPPER DECK WALKWAY

38 Turn L and go F (not U) past the stairs. Then turn L to see the burned section of the port-side deck. Hear that scary music?

Day2, April 3, 1996

there

Go F, L and note the eerie human figures silhouetted in white on the hull. (This gives you the White Shadows Idea icon for later conversations.)

Go L, F, R to the stairs. (You can also return to the interior stairs in the corridor just outside the crew cabins.)

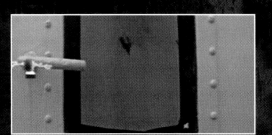

At the stairs, go U, 2F, L, and open the door to the wheelhouse.

WHEELHOUSE

Go 2F, L to find Detective Astadourian.

Before you talk to Astadourian, look at the set of prints on the table next to her. After you back away from the close-up, Astadourian notes fresh fingerprint impressions over dusted prints from the earlier investigation.

Use your Cellular phone to call John Amis. First, select the Cellular phone in the inventory. Use the D-pad arrows to highlight the phone's MENU button, then press ✕ to bring up numbers. Highlight the phone's up-arrow button and press ✕ until you scroll to John Amis's number. Then select the dial button to place the call.

Willmore asks Amis to lift the fresh set of prints.

Talk to Astadourian and use the Payroll Log Idea icon. You have a choice of attitudes regarding a translation of the log. We suggest you agree to let her people translate the log, or at least ask nicely if the bureau can handle it. (If you pull rank, you'll be labeled a jerk.)

Use the Lead Sphere Idea icon. This is one of the most entertaining scenes in the game.

48 Use the White Shadows Idea icon. Willmore takes Astadourian down to show her the shadows. Note what they remind her of. Hiroshima?

49 Return upstairs to the wheelhouse and approach Astadourian again. Officer Mendoza arrives with news from the coroner.

50 Use your PDA to travel to the Coroner's Office in Seattle.

King County Medical Examiner's Office
KING COUNTY, WASHINGTON

51 What a neat place! Browse around. Take in the sights and odors. Kids, can you find the severed hand? (See "Severed hand" in the "Quick Reference" section.)

52 Enter the autopsy room to hear Coroner Truitt's assessment of the tumor-ridden Wong.

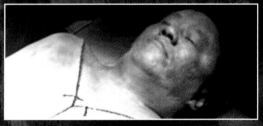

53 Look at Wong's corpse. Did it twitch? If so, you're going down the Paranoia track. (See "UberVariables" in the introduction to the walkthrough.)

54 Click on the organ trays to the right of the coroner for an appetizing close-up. Meat loaf, anyone?

55 Click on the bullet slug near the trays. Willmore asks to take it for analysis, and it appears with your Evidence kit in inventory.

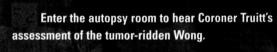

Day2, April 3, 1996

out there

37

Talk to the coroner. Ask all questions and use all Idea icons. You learn that Wong was riddled with malignant tumors. When you ask what could have caused cancer like that, Truitt suggests a massive carcinogenic exposure—radioactive materials, for example. As you might expect, this statement triggers the appearance of the *Tarakan* Idea icon.

Use the *Tarakan* Idea icon on the coroner. Here you get an unexpected jolt of knowledge: Two other FBI agents, a man and a woman, were here recently asking Truitt about the *Tarakan* crewmen. In fact, they ordered the bodies exhumed and the FBI woman performed a second autopsy. Now who do you suppose these agents were?

58 Ask "Who were the FBI agents?" Eventually, the coroner offers to show you the exhumed *Tarakan* crewmen … and discovers they're missing. Sure, she's upset. I don't like it when people take my exhumed bodies, either.

59 Talk to Astadourian and ask what she thinks. Eventually, she disgorges her theory about a Russian plutonium-smuggling ring… and Willmore gets himself a new partner.

60 For fun, snoop around Truitt's office a bit before you leave. Her Emerson quote on the desk is a real hoot, if you think about it. Use your PDA to travel to the Seattle Crime Lab.

King County Crime Lab

61 Talk to Amis and ask all questions, then use the Fingerprints Idea icon.

62 Give Amis all evidence—Lead Sphere, Bullet, and (if not handled by Astadourian's SPD translator) the Captain's Journal and Payroll Log from the *Tarakan*. Use the PDA to travel to Willmore's apartment in Seattle.

THE X FILES

Willmore's Apartment

Enter and go F, L, F to approach the work desk. Select the phone (circled here) to get your messages.

You may hear a message from Willmore's ex-wife Barbara, depending on your Loss track choices. You also hear from Amis regarding the fingerprints. No luck, but he suggests you run them against your FBI database; he e-mailed them to you.

Log onto Willmore's computer and select E-mail. Select and read the e-mail message from John Amis. Use the D-pad arrow to highlight the paper clip icon (TARAKAN.DAT) at bottom, then press X to download the attached file and bring up the ING interface.

Under Search Database, select the FBI button.

Select Search. It's Agent Cook! What are his fingerprints doing in the *Tarakan*?

Click on Quit. When you log off the computer, someone knocks on the door. Go to the door and open it. Guess who?

Agent Cook is a little edgy. He thinks guys in a sedan are following him. Preposterous!

Select any Emotion icon to respond to his accusations. After he spouts his theory about bureau corruption, ask Cook all questions. Remember the UberVariables—some responses are skeptical, others believing. If you feel paranoid, lie to him. He sure wants you to keep him informed, doesn't he?

Use the Fingerprints Idea icon on Cook. This triggers a monologue about smugglers and high bureau officials. And you thought *you* were paranoid! Use the PDA to travel to the Dockside Warehouse in Seattle.

Day 2, April 3, 1996

39

Dockside Warehouse

72 From your supersecret stake-out spot you can see a large hauling truck from Gordon's Hauling, Charno parked by the warehouse door. Time to investigate.

73 Approach the truck and enter the cab on the driver's side.

74 Don't start the engine! Turn R and look at the glove compartment (circled here) for a close-up.

75 Open the glove compartment.

76 Grab the scrap of paper with the address: RR#1121, 82434. (See "1121" in the "Quick Reference" section.)

77 Uh-oh. Exiting the close-up of the scrap triggers the return of the truck driver.

78 Quickly! Go R, F to hop out of the truck cab on the passenger's side.

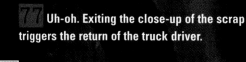

79 Use the PDA to get the e-mail from the Harbor Master, Dan Zirlin. He has the Majestic Shipping phone numbers you requested. Then use the PDA to travel to Willmore's apartment.

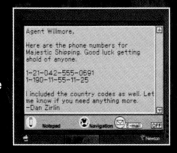

Agent Willmore,

Here are the phone numbers for Majestic Shipping. Good luck getting ahold of anyone.

1-21-042-555-0691
1-190-11-55-11-25

I included the country codes as well. Let me know if you need anything more.
-Dan Zirlin

Willmore's Apartment

80 Go into the bedroom and select Willmore's bed to sleep.

THE X FILES

APRIL 4 1996

Willmore's Apartment

1 Good morning, Craig. Care to start off your day with some gruesome burn footage?

2 Detective Astadourian has big news. Talk to her and ask all questions to learn about the "John Doe," a truck driver for Gordon's Hauling in Charno. Sound familiar? After you ask the last question, the videotape of the "thing" plays automatically.

Chatsworth, CA. lot 112560

REC   4/4/96 6:17am

3 Pretty standard surveillance stuff. There's Mulder's rental car. There's the driver, emerging. Now there's the truck guy from the warehouse last night. And look—there's a high-intensity burst of radioactivity emitting from the driver's intestinal area. Wait. Maybe that last thing is sort of unusual.

NOTE

Is it Mulder in the videotape? Willmore assumes so, but *The X-Files* fans will watch the videotape over and over and, after much Internet debate, conclude that no, it is not Mulder.

4 After you watch the videotape, Astadourian asks for your opinion. Select any answer. (A "believer" will acknowledge the "body light." A skeptic will suspect something else, such as a weapon.) You automatically receive a fax from Amis in your machine.

5 If you had the FBI translate the Cyrillic Payroll Log and Captain's Journal from the *Tarakan*, use your Cellular phone to call Amis at the Crime Lab. He faxes you that translation, too. However, if you let the Seattle PD do the work, Astadourian tells you about Wong and shows you a copy of the log/journal translation.

NOKIA

JOHN AMIS

2065550171

Mikhail Ditkovskaya	95/5	$220
Cheng Yee	95/5	$205
Alexi Gorayeb	95/5	$200
Andrey Korchinsky	95/5	$140
Michael Tong	95/5	$120
James Wong	95/5	$220
Alex Natalenko	95/5	$190
Konstantin Urbanik	95/5	$200
Mikhail Merdanovic	95/5	$150
Alex Natalenko	95/6	$190
Alexi Gorayeb	95/6	$200
James Wong	95/6	$220
Konstantin Urbanik	95/6	$200
Valeri Zirnovksy	95/6	$180
Mikhail Merdanovic	95/6	$160
Mirek Kreicheck	95/6	$200
Vladimir Norchenko	95/6	$220

6 Examine the translation fax (if you have it). Ah, so Wong *was* on the *Tarakan* payroll.

is acting up like last voyage. Latitude 41N, Longitude 158E. 2000km to destination.

3.12.96
Ninth day out, as storm continued through morning, though worst has passed. The seas roll with white waves and much churning is to continue as winds persist. Crew remains good natured. Round of vodka at dinner this eve. There is little to do today. Ship maintenance is continuing, though no problems encountered. All stores inventoried, no depletion beyond normal. Latitude 44N, Longitude138E, 1270 km to destination.

3.13.96
Tenth day out. What can be described as Aurora Borealis lights seen in sky by myself, First Mate Scriabin and Mate Korchinsky. The light, extremely bright and

Read the Captain's Journal translation, too. Note the odd entry about bright lights in the sky, which the *Tarakan*'s Captain attributes to the aurora borealis.

Talk to Astadourian and use all four Idea icons: Gordon's Hauling, *Tarakan*, Crew Cut Man, and Mulder. She's pretty set on her smuggling theory, isn't she?

Go L, F to the work desk and get the fax(es) from the fax machine (circled here).

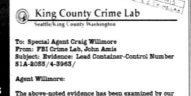

King County Crime Lab
Seattle/King County Washington

To: Special Agent Craig Willmore
From: FBI Crime Lab, John Amis
Subject: Evidence: Lead Container-Control Number S1A-2055/4-3963/

Agent Willmore:

The above-noted evidence has been examined by our laboratory and the following conclusions can be drawn:

This is an industrial-grade lead container of undetermined manufacture, apparently used for the transportation of hazardous nuclear material(s).

Examine the fax(es). Amis's analysis of the Lead Sphere container reports is most interesting.

Don't forget to share any FBI info with your partner. If you had the bureau translate the Payroll Log and Captain's Journal, give Astadourian that translation fax. Also give Astadourian the fax from Amis with the Lead Sphere analysis. That settles it for her; yep, Russian mobsters are smuggling plutonium.

NOTE

You can go to Gordon's Hauling in Charno right away, if you want. As Astadourian says, it's a four-hour trip. But don't worry, Coroner Truitt is working late tonight if you choose Charno as your first destination.

Time to saddle up. Ask Astadourian if you can shower first. Then use your PDA to travel to the Coroner's Office in Seattle.

King County Medical Examiner's Office

Ah, another jolly visit to Coroner Truitt. This new corpse is even more nauseating than Wong's. Truitt points out the poor fellow's "Hiroshima-like radiation exposure." Poor guy goes to his grave with "Gordon's Hauling" forever burned to his chest.

14 Talk to the coroner and ask all questions. Note her comment about inverse shadows etched into walls by the thermic rays of the Hiroshima bomb. Note also her speculation that burns like these would have to result from "a blast of some sort." Merely mishandling radioactive materials won't cut it.

15 Use your PDA to travel to Gordon's Hauling in Charno.

Gordon's Hauling
CHARNO, WASHINGTON

YARD

16 Willmore and Astadourian arrive at Gordon's Hauling at night. From this entry gate, go F.

17 Open the front door to enter the office.

OFFICE

18 Go F into the office straight ahead.

19 Turn R and look D to see the logbook on the office floor. Look at the logbook for a close-up.

20 Pick up the logbook to trigger a brutal attack by a man with serious corneal abnormalities.

The intruder tosses Willmore and Astadourian aside like rag dolls, and then runs out, locking the door behind him. Trapped!

Forget the wire cutters in the toolbox by the shovel! The only place you can use them is on the bomb itself, which will then explode.

And things get worse. Astadourian finds a bomb in a file cabinet! It's ready to explode in seconds.

23 Door's locked; bomb's ticking. Now what? Quickly! Look at the shovel (circled here, just left of the bomb file cabinet) for a close-up.

Quickly! Take the shovel.

Turn L to face the refrigerator, then look D at the grate (circled here) next to the refrigerator. Quickly! Use the shovel to open the grate.

If the Grate Escape succeeds, Willmore and Astadourian get out just in the nick of time.

If your attempt fails, however, you go up in smoke—along with the Cigarette-Smoking Man's latest Morley.

NOTE

If you die, you see the brief shot of the Cigarette-Smoking Man only if you found both Morley cigarette butts earlier in the game—one on the floor of the dockside warehouse, the other next to Wong's dead body outside the warehouse.

Yard

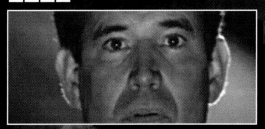

Someone's watching.

That was close. But there's nothing like a narrow escape from death to get the old hormones flowing. Go ahead. Try to kiss Astadourian.

Talk with Astadourian and use all Idea icons. She thinks the bomb was meant to trap and kill someone. But who was the target? You or the eye guy? Travel to Willmore's apartment in Seattle.

Willmore's Apartment

Site: Apt: Trans. of payroll log/Tarakan: Wong's name on list of payees. Asta: maybe W. killed by mob after questioning by me. Putting the guilt trip on me!
Shows vid tape: gas station surveillance – dark–haired man in 95 Taurus Lic: 621517–Wash. – Same as car rented by Agts. Mulder & Scully from Lariat Rental. Bright flash, picture blank. Victim suffered burns matching Tarakan sailors. John Doe (crewcut man) died at scene.

Notepad   Navigation   E-mail   OFF

Just to get Willmore's perspective on all these recent and troubling incidents, open inventory and select the PDA. Press ● to highlight the Notepad pencil icon at the bottom. Press ✕ to select the Notepad, press ● to bring up the scroll arrows, then use the direction pad to scroll through Willmore's notes.

Scully. Both work out of Bureau HQ in D.C. No trace of them has been found, but we're running down some leads. If I'm successful in finding them, it would look good in my file.

I was hoping to get some time off this weekend, but now with the Big Gun from the Bureau in town it doesn't seem likely, not even for Easter Sunday. I'll have to make it up to Elizabeth later

Go into the bedroom and read the latest entries in Willmore's journal on the nightstand. Then select the bed to sleep.

Day 4

Willmore's Apartment

After Willmore awakens, use your PDA to travel to the FBI Field Office in Seattle.

FBI Field Office

Go R, F to enter the meeting room. Approach Agent Cook, who's prepping for a raid. What's up, Mark?

Talk to Cook and ask all questions. He has all the answers, doesn't he?

An excited Cook tells Willmore he's cracked the case. A known Georgian smuggler named Yvgeny Smolnikoff operates out of a warehouse in Seattle. (His photo appears in your inventory.) Cook also claims to have a witness who can place Smolnikoff at the warehouse dock on the night of Wong's murder. A Seattle SWAT unit is on the way for backup.

Use your PDA to travel to Smolnikoff's Warehouse in Seattle.

Rainier Cold Storage (Smolnikoff's Warehouse)
SEATTLE, WASHINGTON

According to Cook, "surveillance" reported that Smolnikoff entered the building alone. Cowboy Mark doesn't want to wait for SWAT backup. Better be careful.

In the inventory, click on your SIG-Sauer P226 9mm automatic. (For the technically challenged, this is your "gun.")

After you select the gun, note that when you move the pointer back onto the viewing area, it becomes a crosshair for targeting purposes.

If you don't have the Action Scene Auto-Rewind feature enabled in the Options menu, turn it on now. Or else save your game here.

Be sure Cook provides cover fire before you swing into harm's way. (See the next step.) Otherwise, you're headline material.

Select Cook with the Action Hand pointer. He fires a few cover rounds into the warehouse.

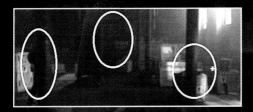

NOTE

The Georgian gunmen appear in random order every time you try the gunfight.

12 Quickly turn R. Three Georgian gunmen, one by one, pop out from behind posts on the first floor. (The positions of all three are circled here.) As each one appears, quickly use the direction pad to move the crosshair pointer over the goon and press ✕ to shoot. (Again, be sure your gun is active in inventory.) When you hit a gunman, the crosshair flashes red.

13 After you clear the first floor, keep your gun active (you should see the crosshairs onscreen) and go 2F toward the stairs at the back left of the main floor.

14 From the bottom of the stairs, go F, L, U, F to climb to the second floor. Again, be sure your gun is drawn.

15 Quickly! Turn 2R and nail the Georgian goon sneaking up behind you.

16 Quickly! Turn 2R (or 2L) and blast the Georgian goon behind the slatted doorway. (Apparently, he thinks those door slats provide cover.)

17 From the slatted doorway, turn 2R and go F (not D), 2R, U, and 2F to see the winding staircase on the third floor (shown here).

18 Go F, L, D (circled here, just left of the winding stairs), and then F to head down the back stairs to Smolnikoff's lair.

SMOLNIKOFF'S LAIR

19 Don't shoot Smolnikoff! Cook finally appears and tells you to secure the place. Sure, why not? Cook says he spotted a .38 caliber gun downstairs, back-left corner.

20 Holster your gun. (Just press ▲.) Time for some possibly tricky navigation. Go F, L, U, F to climb the back stairs to the third floor. Go R, F (through the doorway), F (across the catwalk), D, F to the second floor. Go 2R, F (not U), 2R, D, F, R, D, F to the first floor. You should end up facing the warehouse front door (as shown here) leading outside.

FIRST FLOOR

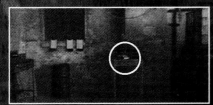

21 Go R, F, R, F to see the payroll manifest (circled here) on the table.

22 Look at the manifest for a close-up. Looks like the one you found aboard the *Tarakan*. Surely it will prove interesting to some FBI budget analyst somewhere.

23 Turn R and look at the black eagle emblem (circled here) on the open crate. It's the same one you saw on the *Tarakan*.

24 Go F and look down to see the .38 (circled here) on the floor. Just where Cook said it was.

Take the gun. (It appears in inventory when you highlight your evidence kit.)

Retrace your route all the way back to Smolnikoff's lair. OK, if you really need help: From the gun, go R, F, 2R, F (toward the stairs at left), F (up the stairs), R, U, F (you should see the slatted door), 2R, F, 2R, U, 3F, L, D, F, R to see Cook and Smolnikoff.

SMOLNIKOFF'S LAIR

Talk to Smolnikoff. Ask all the questions and use all the idea icons. He denies everything—smuggling plutonium, shooting Scully, killing Wong and the *Tarakan* crew—and seems genuinely shocked by your accusations.

Note Smolnikoff's response when you use the Warehouse Idea icon. "You're *in* my warehouse!" When you use the Idea icon for Smolnikoff's gun, Cook suggests a ballistics test. Good idea, partner.

Use your PDA to travel to the Crime Lab in Seattle.

Crime Lab

When you enter, note that Amis doesn't feel so good.

Select Smolnikoff's gun to have Amis run a ballistics test. Guess what? The test bullet matches the slugs that hit Scully and Wong. Then travel back to Smolnikoff's Warehouse.

Smolnikoff's Warehouse

You automatically reappear in Smolnikoff's lair if you use your PDA. Talk to Smolnikoff and tell him his gun matches one that shot an FBI agent. Again, he denies everything and Cook hauls him off.

When your cellular phone rings, click on it to answer Amis's unhappy phone call. He's a little hot under the collar—in more ways than one. Use the PDA to travel to Willmore's apartment.

Willmore's Apartment

Shortly after you enter the room you hear a knock on the door. Open the door and brace yourself for a tongue-lashing from Detective Astadourian.

Talk to Astadourian. Tell her you thought she knew about it. Any response you pick triggers a mysterious phone call.

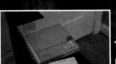

Listen to the message. The anonymous caller claims Mulder and Scully are alive and requests a dawn meeting at Sand Point Hangar 4. (Even casual X-philes will recognize the voice of X.) He also insists "this has nothing to do with Russian smugglers."

After Astadourian leaves, go to the work desk. You can select the answering machine to listen to the message again. Then access the computer and click on "E-mail." Open the e-mail message from Otto Dee.

Scroll down to the bottom of the e-mail message to highlight the attached file (JOHN-DOE.DAT), then press X to download the fingerprints of the crew-cut truck driver. They automatically load into the ING interface.

Select the button next to "Government/Military" and then select "Search." Restricted data? Hmmm. Don't tell me he's a government man.

Quit the computer and go to the bedroom. Activate your PDA and click on the pencil icon to read Willmore's latest field notes. Then click on the bed to sleep.

Day 5

Willmore's Apartment

After you wake up, use your PDA to travel to Sand Point Hangar 4 in Seattle.

Sand Point Naval Station, Hangar 4
SEATTLE, WASHINGTON

Willmore arrives in a big, empty hangar with a really wet floor. Those Navy guys sure know how to mop.

Turn 3R to see two open doorways. Go F through the door on the right (circled here).

Meet X. Choose any Emotion icon.

X insists you tell no one about this meeting. When he asks for your word, be smart and select "You have my word." According to X, lives are at stake here, including your own. He says Mulder and Scully are still alive, but they aren't together. He suggests you find the "Jane Doe" who checked into the Presbyterian Hospital in Gold Bar three days ago.

Then X gives you an odd-looking stiletto and says it's possible to kill the man you must find only by inserting this blade into the base of his neck. "This man is not what he seems," X adds. "If the injury is not precise, he will kill you."

Don't follow X! If you do, Craig gets to push up daisies and you get to reload a saved game.

Instead, turn in either direction to trigger Astadourian's appearance. It gives Craig a bit of a shock … but it looks like the partnership is back on.

Use your PDA to travel to the hospital in Gold Bar.

Presbyterian Hospital
GOLD BAR, WASHINGTON
HALLWAY

10 Meet Dr. McIntyre. She's friendly enough, but she doesn't trust you any further than she can throw you. So remember, honesty is always the best policy. (Unless, of course, you're NSA.)

11 Tell Dr. McIntyre you're looking for Dana Scully.

12 Tell Dr. McIntyre you're with the FBI. Then show the good doctor your FBI badge.

13 When she asks for the name of Scully's superior, again, tell the truth—Walter Skinner. Now you can talk to the doctor and ask all questions, then go F past her to Scully's room.

SCULLY'S ROOM

14 At last, Dana Scully—she's a bit weak, but she's still sharp as an alien stiletto. And as you might imagine, she's a little wary of people who burst into the room looking for her.

15 She's also packing heat, so be straight with her, or she senses a liar and you get the business end of her weapon. First, tell her Assistant Director Skinner asked you to look for her. Then tell her you're Agent Willmore.

THE X FILES

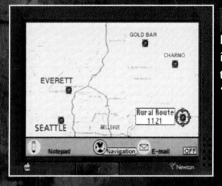

16 When Scully asks who told you she was here, press ▲ to remove the dialogue options, and then press ● to bring up your inventory. (Be quick! Scully takes no chances.) Highlight the stiletto from X and press ✕ to select it.

17 Talk with Scully about the case. Ask all the questions and use all the Idea icons. (You can also show her the Smolnikoff photo.)

18 Use your PDA to travel to Rural Route 1121. True X-Files fans will grasp immediately the insider significance of this rural route address. (See "1121" in "*The X-Files* Quick Reference.")

Rural Route 1121: Rail Yard
GOLD BAR, WASHINGTON

19 So what are you looking for here? Remember the address on the paper scrap from the glove compartment of the Gordon's Hauling delivery truck? It included the number 82434. That's not a zip code, friend.

20 Go 9F between the rows of boxcars to the bottom of the old power pole. Look U to see the top of the pole. Bet it's a nice view from there.

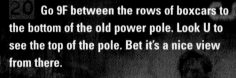

21 Climb the pole. Craig's pretty spry for a guy in a trench coat.

22 At the top, turn once (L or R). Then open your inventory and highlight the binoculars.

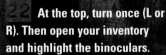
Binoculars

23 Press ✕ to select the binoculars and view boxcar number 82434. (See "82434" in "*The X-Files* Quick Reference.")

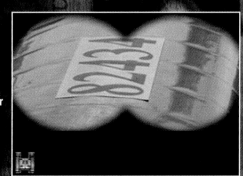

Press ▲ to de-select your binoculars, then go D the pole. Detective Astadourian waits for you at the bottom. Talk to her and ask all questions.

25 Go R, F (stepping between cars), R, 2F and look at the door (circled here) of the boxcar on the right.

26 Astadourian notes the burned boxcar. Go F past her (on the far left) and open the boxcar door.

27 Willmore and Astadourian enter the burned-out, smoky boxcar (serial number 82434). Astadourian points out that the fire was recent.

28 Go F to the charred mess in the next room. Astadourian suggests it looks like "an operating room of some kind."

29 Go 2R, 2F (past Astadourian) to exit the boxcar. This triggers the appearance of the homeless flossing man.

30 Talk to the man and ask all questions. Eventually, he admits he found "stuff" in the burned boxcar. When he asks you to guess what stuff he has, select the following in this order: Photographs, Moving Pictures, Videotape.

31 Finally, the nut case gives Don and Jane a videotape ... for a modest fee. Use your PDA to travel back to the Seattle Field Office.

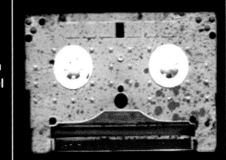

52

FBI Field Office

If you travel here with the boxcar videotape, Willmore and Astadourian automatically go to Willmore's desk.

Select the videotape from inventory and put it in the VCR slot just to the right of the desktop computer (circled here). Agent Cook automatically joins the audience.

The videotape shows some sort of suspicious medical procedure conducted in the boxcar. An autopsy?

Then Willmore freezes a video frame showing a face in the foreground. Hey, that's the oily-eyed guy who attacked him at the Charno hauling yard. Willmore asks, "If this guy's a surgeon, what was he looking for at Gordon's Hauling?" Craig asks all the right questions, doesn't he?

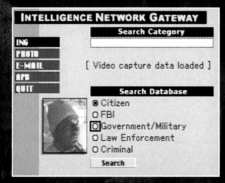

Press ✕ to select "Capture" on the Photo Viewer screen. Under "Search Database," click on the Government/Military button.

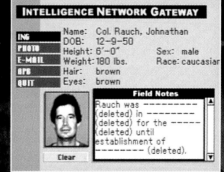

Click on "Search." The subject is Jonathan Rauch, a navy surgeon with a heavily deleted, highly classified record. Note his assignments to Eisenhower Field in Alaska, a medical facility in Perky, West Virginia, and something called Operation Black Cloak.

Select "Quit" to exit the computer. When the videoconferencing link request automatically appears, press ✕ to select "Connect."

Talk with Byers, Frohike, and Langly—the infamous Lone Gunmen—and ask all questions. (See "Lone Gunmen" in *The X-Files* Quick Reference.") The guys explain that Agent Scully asked them to provide help. They believe a top-secret facility in Alaska is storing an alien spacecraft recovered from the Pacific Ocean.

NOTE

During his conversation with the Lone Gunmen, Willmore absorbs some classic *X-Files* mythology—for example, "boxcar work," a massive network of railcars where secret government medical units conduct genetic experiments to promote the "cross-pollinization" of human and alien species.

After the Lone Gunmen sign off, Cook takes charge and travel plans are made. Detective Astadourian's attitude toward Willmore's trip to Alaska varies significantly, reflecting the nature of their relationship at this point.

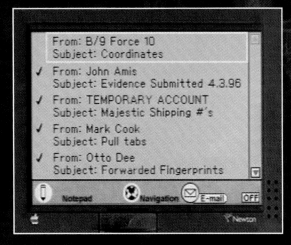

Use your PDA to open the e-mail from "B/9 Force 10."

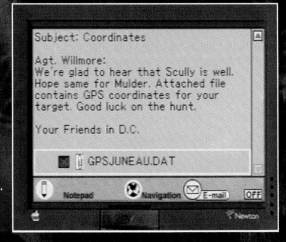

42 Scroll down to the bottom of the message and press ✕ to select the flashing paper clip icon (GPSJUNEAU.DAT). This downloads the GPS (Global Positioning System) Alaska coordinates, adding "Rauch's House" to your PDA Navigation map.

43 Use your PDA to travel to Rauch's House in Alaska.

Day 6

APRIL 7,1996

Rauch's House
OUTSIDE JUNEAU, ALASKA

Hey, who was that guy in black? It wasn't Rauch, and he sure left in a hurry. Let's slip inside the cabin and see what kind of a host Rauch is.

After the mysterious jeep drives away, go F to the porch stairs, then go F again, veering right (shown here) to approach the cabin's front door.

Go F toward the door. Open the door to enter the cabin.

INTERIOR

Inside the front door, turn R. Then climb the stairs by going F, L, F. At the top of the stairs, turn L to see Rauch slimed on the floor.

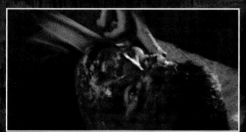

Try to talk to Rauch. No luck. He isn't being a very good host.

Look at the cord (circled here) hanging from the ceiling near the desk.

In the close-up, grab the cord to pull down the ladder to the attic. Go F to climb into the attic.

ATTIC

Meet Fox Mulder. He's kind of tied up at the moment, but Willmore quickly disentangles that problem. Now maybe you can get some straight answers.

Talk to Mulder. Ask all questions. Mulder's answers are pretty fantastic, aren't they? He explains "Valdez-type aliens," oily eyes, getting flamed, and other odd phenomena associated with this X-File.

Day6, April 7, 1996

55

Rauch, it turns out, wasn't really Rauch but an alien entity inhabiting Rauch's body. A species of alien uses the human body as a host. Apparently, this viscous parasite enters its host through any available orifice. (Fans of the television series will recognize the species from its first appearance in the "Piper Maru" and "Apocrypha" episodes of the third season.)

The parasite inhabits the target human, gaining access to the human's knowledge base—in effect, merging its identity with its host's. As Mulder sees it, the crew of the *Tarakan* picked up one of these "Valdez-type aliens" and got nuked by the creature's ability to emit powerful radioactive thermic rays.

Somehow, the government captured the alien and conducted medical experiments in boxcar 82434. But then, as Mulder puts it, "somebody screwed up and it escaped." Who screwed up? Take a guess. Remember the videotape of the boxcar operating room? Didn't Rauch remove his protective facial gear before moving off-screen? Oops. And now it seems the alien has a new host—the man in black who just left as Willmore arrived.

Another noteworthy bit of information: Mulder explains that the only difference between a normal human being and a parasite host is the thin film of black oil swimming over the victim's eyes. You might want to keep that in mind.

When your cell phone rings, select the phone in inventory to take Scully's phone call.

11 After Mulder finishes his conversation with Scully, NSA agents appear outside. Mulder asks you to distract them, and then meet up with him at the secret government facility. Sure, Fox!

12 Go R, D, F to exit the attic. Go R, F, R, F, R, F to get back downstairs. Turn R and go F to exit the cabin through the front door.

EXTERIOR (PORCH)

13 Time for action. Go R, F to proceed to the front corner of the porch, near the cars. You face the two men.

14 One of the spooky men identifies himself as an NSA agent and tells you your investigation here is over.

They've come to escort you to the airport. What nice guys! You can avoid this "escort" in either of two ways, depending on your mood and proclivities.

TO KILL THE NSA GOONS (AND AVOID THE WOODS ESCAPE SEQUENCE)

15 Don't move forward! Click on your gun. Willmore draws and aims.

16 Quickly! Shoot either agent. You see him fall. Quickly! Shoot the other agent. Then select your vehicle at the left. Willmore automatically travels to the secret Alaskan facility.

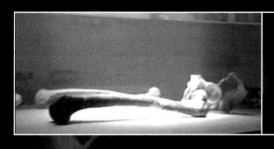

Don't let this happen to you. If the NSA spooks get the drop on you, Truitt identifies your bones, and Cook lights up. You don't suppose that's a Morley he's smoking, do you?

TO RUN AWAY FROM THE NSA GOONS:

18 Don't move forward! Turn right. Move the pointer until it becomes the Action Hand icon. Click to run away into the woods. (To escape, see the next section.)

WOODS (OUTSIDE RAUCH'S HOUSE)

If you killed the NSA men back at the house, you won't have to complete the following steps. Note also that, if you're feeling frisky, you can turn and engage your pursuers in a gunfight at any time during the woods chase.

19 Willmore sprints through the dark trees with the NSA killers hot on his trail.

20 After Willmore stops running, go R, 2F, and click on the hollow (circled here) under the big tree root to hide.

After the NSA agents head off in another direction, Willmore automatically sprints to the car and drives away. You automatically travel to the secret Alaskan base.

Secret Base, Alaska

Well, that aurora borealis sure is gorgeous. And what's that lovely odor? Roasted flesh, isn't it?

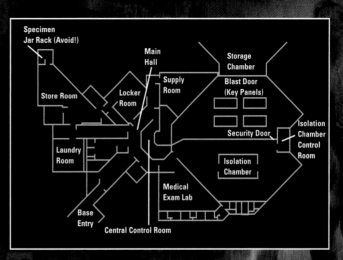

21 Here's a map of the secret base. You can find the same map on some of the facility's monitors. Of course, here we've thoughtfully labeled each important room.

BASE ENTRY/MAIN HALLWAY

You begin in an entry hall with Scully, who examines yet another burn victim. Clearly, our boy's here. Scully says Mulder went on ahead. Let's go find him.

Draw your gun when you enter the facility and be ready to use it. Hostile soldiers roam the hallways.

From the entry room where you meet Scully, go F into the next room. (Scully appears again. Note the reverse shadows on the wall.) Go F through the door into the main hallway.

When you enter the main hallway, you face the interior windows of the Central Control Room, where a bunch of flickering monitors crackle and hiss. (Check the map to see how the facility is laid out.)

Turn L and go 2F down the hallway, keeping close to the right-hand wall. (You can also go F toward some of the doorways as you move down the hall, but for this walkthrough, stick close to the right wall.)

Turn L to look in the open door. You should see a burned soldier (circled here) on the floor beyond the doorway.

Keep your gun drawn and ready. You'll need it in a moment. Go F to enter the Locker Room.

Turn R to see Mulder. Uh-oh. Lots more charbroiled corpses, plus Mulder's looking a little oily-eyed. He's being a good host in a bad sort of way.

LOCKER ROOM (MULDER)

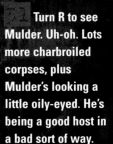

Mulder picks up a key and tells Scully he needs two keys to open the blast doors into the Storage Chamber. What could Mulder want in the Storage Chamber? The answer: Nothing. But the killer alien swimming through Mulder's system right now would love to get back to its spacecraft.

THE X FILES

Why do you need to get into a blast door?
Scully, run!

33 Don't shoot Mulder! It's useless. But keep your gun drawn. After Mulder asks Scully for help, select: "Scully, run!" Willmore automatically turns and runs through the door across the room.

STORE ROOM

34 Here's where you need your gun. A soldier is posted here with his back to you, and he's spooked enough to shoot anything that moves. Quickly! Turn R and shoot the soldier before he turns and fires!

35 Warning! Do *not* turn L and cross the Store Room past the barrels to the racks of specimen jars. If you reach the position shown here ...

36 ... you're doomed. An alien-controlled Scully will kill you when you turn in either direction.

37 Instead, turn R and open the door to go back into the Locker Room. (Don't worry, Mulder is gone.)

LOCKER ROOM

38 Look at the guy in the oil spill on the floor. That's the man in black fatigues you saw running from Rauch's cabin. Like Rauch, he's now an ex-host. That explains Mulder's oily gaze and all the flamed soldiers strewn about.

39 Turn R to see this row of lockers, then go 2F into the main hallway.

MAIN HALLWAY

40 Again, you face the windows of the Central Control Room. You have a task to perform in there, but not yet. Let's go find Scully first.

Turn L and go F through the doorway (circled here).

Go 2F down the short hall and turn R to face the Supply Room doorway (shown here). Go F to enter the Supply Room. Warning! Another soldier lurks nearby. Read on to find out where.

SUPPLY ROOM

NOTE

This visit to the Supply Room is optional. You don't have to come here to win the game.

Turn R twice to see Scully examine controls in a glassed-in control room. She emerges and talks to Willmore about Mulder's odd behavior.

TALK   HISTORY
I think he's looking for what's being stored at this facility.
He said he was looking for ▼

Go ahead, talk to Scully. But before you make your dialog selection, know that your conversation (regardless of choice) will end prematurely with the sudden appearance of a hostile base guard behind you.

Your best tactic? Make your dialog choice, then *immediately* select your gun from inventory.

Gun

Quickly! Move the gunsight to the position shown here (right over Scully's nose) during the dialog exchange between Willmore and Scully. The conversation ends abruptly when Scully sees the soldier behind you.

But if your gunsight is properly positioned, the soldier steps right into your line of fire. When he does, simply press ✕ to gun down the attacker.

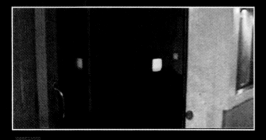

Where'd Scully go? Let's find her again. Go F, L, 2F to return to the Main Hallway. That's the doorway to the Central Control Room directly ahead. But again, we'll visit later. For now, turn R.

Go F, L, 3F down the main hallway. (Again, you can go F into some of the doorways, but stick as close as you can to the left wall this time.)

50 You move around the Central Control Room to the entrance (shown here) of the Isolation Chamber area. But before you enter, let's take care of some unfinished business with your buddy, Agent Cook.

51 Turn R to face the entrance to the Medical Examination Lab (shown here). Go 2F to enter the lab. Warning: Prepare for a life-or-death showdown. And save your game here.

MEDICAL EXAMINATION LAB
Showdown with Agent Cook

Wow. What sort of gruesome experiments go on here?

52 Turn R to see the cattle prod (circled here) on the metal table at the far end of the room.

Pick up the cattle prod.

55 This triggers the unwelcome appearance of Agent Cook. Cook abuses you a bit, and if you do nothing, he kills you—all for money. Can you imagine a government employee motivated by greed? Unthinkable. This is not a good ending, of course.

56 You can shoot Cook before he shoots you. But either way, you lose. Why? Because you need Cook alive for the endgame sequence.

57 So rather than resort to crude gunplay, be creative. When Cook stands over you, quickly move the pointer over the cattle prod (circled here) jutting from the end of the table. Click when the pointer becomes the Action Hand.

58 Willmore grabs the prod and jabs it into Cook, rendering him unconscious.

59 To exit the lab, go R, F through the doorway. Then go F again, veering right (as shown here) into the Main Hallway. In the Main Hallway, turn R and go F to enter the Isolation Chamber area.

ISOLATION CHAMBER AREA

60 A small, glassed-in Isolation Chamber sits in the middle of this large open room. Looks like a nice, safe place to keep an alien-infested host.

61 Go 4F along the left side of the Isolation Chamber to the open doorway on the other side of the room.

62 Go F through the open doorway.

ISOLATION CHAMBER CONTROL ROOM

63 Here's Agent Scully again. Listen carefully to her plan.

Scully wants to use the key Mulder seeks to lure him into the Isolation Chamber until she can figure out how to treat him. She points out an adjacent room where a blast door protects the Storage Chamber. The blast door has two key panels; the door opens only if two people insert a key in each panel and turn the keys simultaneously. A key guard sits there with the second key—the one sought by the alien controlling Mulder. Unfortunately, the security door to that area is locked.

So Scully's two-part plan is this: Power up the Isolation Chamber to prepare it for Mulder. Then unlock the security door to the blast door area outside the Storage Chamber. And how do we carry out this plan? Follow me!

After Scully lays out her plan, look at the control panel just left of her (circled here).

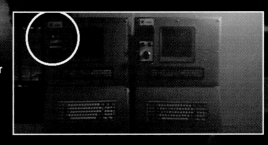

You see a close-up of the Isolation Chamber controls. Look at the green knob (circled here) at the upper left to get an even closer view.

Pull the green knob to power up the Isolation Chamber.

Back away from the close-up, then turn L and go F to exit the control room.

ISOLATION CHAMBER AREA

Now you need to open *both* Isolation Chamber doors. Go L, F to the nearest Isolation Chamber door.

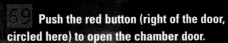

Push the red button (right of the door, circled here) to open the chamber door.

Go R, F, L, 2F, L, F, L to the other chamber door. Again, push the red button (right of the door) to open the second chamber door. Remember, both doors must be opened.)

Turn around (2R) and go F through the doorway (shown here).

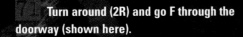

Then go 6F down the main hallway, sticking close to the right-side wall. At the end of the hall, go R, F to enter the Central Control Room—the room with all the monitors on the fritz.

CENTRAL CONTROL ROOM

After you enter the room, go F, L to see the blast door control button (circled here).

Look at the button for a close-up. It's labeled "Life Support Systems: Entry." Then push the button. This opens the security door to the room where the blast doors protect the alien craft in the Storage Area.

Optional: To find a map of the base, use the big monitor (circled) in the center of the control station and select Map from the menu. Of course, you already have access to a labeled map at the beginning of this section.

```
[menu] (srxxBB iu366
>password protected
>all entry attempts recorded

Perimeter Alarm
All Access
Visitor Verification
Confinement Crew
Map
Default Mech
Alert Systems
Early Response Team
Damage Control
Communications
Subsystems Maintenance & Repair
```

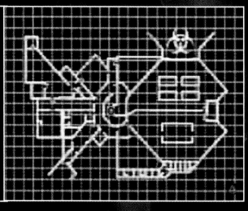

Now you must retrace your route back to the Isolation Chamber area. From the "Life Support Systems: Entry" control button, go L, 2F into the main hallway. In the main hallway, turn L and go F, L, 7F (keeping left) all the way past the Isolation Chamber.

ISOLATION CHAMBER AREA

You should be facing the Isolation Chamber Control Room door again. Don't enter the control room. Instead, turn L to face the security door (now open). Go F to enter the room.

STORAGE CHAMBER (BLAST DOORS)

78 Get ready for the grand finale. Agent Scully has preceded you into the security area near the blast doors. She asks if you'd like to claim any particular direction.

79 Turn R and draw your gun.

80 Go 2F and shoot the poor key guard at the blast door. (Don't shoot Mulder!)

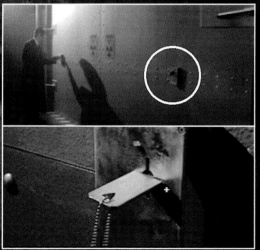

81 Quickly! Take the guard's key from the key slot (circled here).

82 Quickly! Run from the alien-infused Mulder by going L, 4F to the Isolation Chamber.

ISOLATION CHAMBER AREA

83 Now the alien's mad. And he's right on your tail. So complete the following steps with alacrity: First, run 2F through the isolation chamber. Hurry.

84 Turn around (2R) to face the door. Here comes Flame Boy! But look. Scully's behind him at the other door. Quickly! Hit the red button to shut the Isolation Chamber door.

85 Scully closes the far door of the Isolation Chamber, trapping host Mulder and his unwanted visitor.

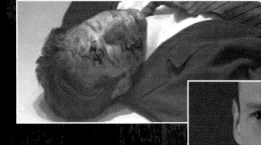

36 Unfortunately, the alien oozes out of Mulder, somehow escapes the chamber, and then enters Cook ...

... who grabs our hero by the throat and forces him to the blast door key slot.

Agent Scully manages to slip in unnoticed behind Cook, but she's powerless without a certain weapon that happens to be in your possession.

89 Quickly! Select the stiletto from your inventory.

90 Quickly! Click the stiletto on Scully to toss it to her.

Scully knows exactly what to do with the alien blade, and wastes no time doing it.

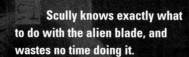

92 And both Agent Cook and his "tenant" meet an oily end. Congratulations, my friend. You've won the game.

THE X FILES

1 The next evening brings Agent Willmore back from Alaska to the Seattle Field Office of the FBI.

FBI FIELD OFFICE, SEATTLE

2 Director Shanks and Agent Scully congratulate Agent Willmore on a job well done. Both note that Willmore's work has merited the special attention of Assistant Director Skinner back in Washington, D.C.

And it gets better: Shanks mentions that Detective Mary Astadourian has some "paperwork" to drop off at Willmore's apartment.

NOTE

Needless to say, Detective Astadourian won't have "some forms for you to sign" if you were a pompous jerk during the game.

As Agent Willmore approaches the front entrance of the Eavelyn Apartments, the mysterious X pays him an unexpected visit. Willmore assumes X wants his stiletto back.

But X suggests Agent Willmore keep it awhile longer. "You're going to need it again," he says. "Soon."

An Interview with Greg Roach

Greg Roach is the co-founder, CEO, and Artistic Director of HyperBole Studios, the development house that created *The X-Files* game for Fox Interactive. Although he's quick to share credit with all involved, Roach is undoubtedly the project's kinetic center—besides running his company, he co-designed the game elements, wrote the shooting script, directed the primary live-action sequences, and was lead editor during postproduction. Plus, his shadow is a black hole capable of atomically unzipping matter into pure energy. Fortunately, the following conversation took place via phone.

Roach's HyperBole Studios, of course, is no newcomer to interactive media. Founded in 1990, HyperBole is perhaps best known as a pioneer of the live-action genre. Groundbreaking titles such as *Quantum Gate* and *The Vortex* set the early standards for live-action games. Those two products, says Roach, laid the groundwork for *The X-Files* game, both in terms of developing HyperBole's VirtualCinema technology and attracting the attention of Fox Interactive.

Gillian chats with D.P. Jon Joffin.

Barba: Let's start with some background about yourself. How did you get into the industry?

Roach: Well, first, HyperBole Studios would like to thank everyone at Fox Interactive for their courage and perseverance in making this project a reality. In answer to your question, I'm not really a technologist. My training is as a director. I have an MFA from the University of Houston, where I also did my undergraduate work. After graduate school, I was perfectly happy with my career directing in theater and film. I got interested in the computer as a creative tool, a storytelling tool; I certainly never thought it would turn into a business. But one day I got a wild hair and proposed an online magazine to some writers I was hanging out with back in the late 1980s. We did it free for a few months, then a publisher picked it up and we formed a company.

The response was quite positive, and I also began to see other creative possibilities using the medium. So I began devoting full-time to HyperBole, and never looked back.

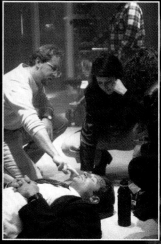

Greg Roach, David Duchovny, Anji Bemben (make-up artist), and Laverne Basham (hair stylist).

Barba: Tell us about the genesis of *The X-Files* project.

Roach: Fox approached us about three years ago, wondering if we were interested in the project. I hate to say it now, but we initially turned them down (laughs). I'd never seen *The X-Files* at that point; it hadn't really taken off yet, although it certainly had a core following of loyal fans from the very beginning. But then I watched the show. The creative possibilities were intriguing, so we went back to Fox and affirmed our interest.

We had to compete with a number of other companies, submitting a series of proposals and prototypes and so forth. After six or seven months we managed to prove to Fox and Ten Thirteen Productions [creators of the TV series] that we were the right folks for the job. After that, we met with Ten Thirteen. Chris [Carter, creator of the series] and Frank [Spotnitz, one of the show's core writer/producers] gave us a story outline.

Interestingly, way back then they already knew how the overarching story, their "mythology," would play out over the next few years. And we thought: "Now, that's really cool!"

Barba: It's incredible, really. That vision is one of the core secrets of Ten Thirteen's success with the TV series. It's unique, the way the mythology has woven its way through several seasons and continues to build.

Roach: That vision let our game fit into the stuff that's happening now with the series and the upcoming feature film [released on June 19, 1998]. Even though our story is set in the "past" [between the third and fourth seasons], the black-oil alien still interlocks perfectly with where the series has gone and with the feature film. It's really remarkable that they had such a grasp of where they were taking things.

Barba: So how did the story-development process work?

Roach: After we got the story outline from Chris Carter, we spent some time going back and forth, fleshing it out. We added our input from an interactive standpoint. For example, Chris had some *deus ex machina* story elements, where, say, something happens or an important piece of information or tool is suddenly delivered by some source. Well, we'd say, "That's an important plot point, and in an interactive game the player should earn that piece of information through his choices or actions." So it's not just *delivered*, but *uncovered*.

Barba: So your early focus was on identifying the game elements in Chris Carter's original story.

Roach: Exactly. And Ten Thirteen was really open to that. They accepted the fact that we brought some significant expertise to the project, and they gave us a lot of autonomy in crafting the game elements. On our side, we had great respect for Chris's original story vision, and stayed true to it all the way.

Once we had a story outline that everybody agreed on, our team—Phil Peters, our producer at HyperBole; Paul Hiaumet, our composer and a partner since the beginning; and Cassandria Blackmore, our lead graphics artist—sat down for several months and hammered out all the fine details of the gameplay and the interactive structure. Then I took all the design documents, locked myself in a room, and banged out the script. This whole time, I should add, we were in frequent contact with people at Ten Thirteen—Frank Spotnitz, in particular. He and I spoke almost daily, kicking around story nuances, and Frank would spoon-feed me pieces of *The X-Files* mythology.

Another writer, Richard Dowdy, came aboard as the revisions began. He had a big part in the subsequent writing, of which there is much, as you know. The amount of text in the game—journals, e-mail, the ING, various documents—is enormous. Meanwhile, our technology crew was rebuilding our engine and all of the tools from scratch. After the script felt solid, the preproduction process began to gear up: detailed storyboards, location scouting, costume design, props, etc.

Barba: How much was Ten Thirteen Productions involved once you got to this visualization phase of the project?

Roach: As with the game-design phase, we had great autonomy in our preproduction and production phases. Ten Thirteen was always there for us if we needed them. They provided a guiding aesthetic hand and gave us gracious support. But most of the preproduction design and production work was done by HyperBole. It was a good collaboration.

The next steps, of course, were to plan and execute the shoot itself. We knew our budget would lock us into a limited number of shooting days, and given that we'd end up with about six hours of finished material, we had to be very, very efficient. But I got lucky. Our producer here, Phil Peters, has a ton of experience shooting for television and features, and he knew where to find a really crackerjack crew.

Another constraint, of course, was the reality of David Duchovny's and Gillian Anderson's schedules. But we got them right between finishing the series and starting the feature film. So we got lucky there, too.

Barba: Where did you find the actor, Jordan Lee Williams, who plays Craig Willmore?

Roach: He's a local guy here in Seattle. He auditioned for us. He's since moved to Los Angeles. I think his experience on this project gave him a boost of confidence. He was everybody's first choice.

Barba: I thought he had good chemistry with the Mary Astadourian character (played by Paige Witte).

Roach: Paige actually appeared in our other titles, *Quantum Gate* and *The Vortex*. She did a great job then, too. In fact, she won some acting awards from some of the game magazines. Detective Astadourian's relationship with Agent Willmore is so critical to the emotional life of this story. That may seem odd to say about a game, but then I think that's what *The X-Files* is all about—extremely real, believable characters, with the Mulder-Scully relationship at the center.

Anyway, the next step was full-blown filming. We shot seven weeks total in and around the Seattle area. We did a lot of the filming at a recently decommissioned naval base, Sand Point. It was perfect because we'd worried about the secret NSA facility at the end of the game. It had to be big, it had to be scary, it had to be a Byzantine maze with corridors and machinery. At Sand Point, they'd built a new brig, and then a year later the base was shut down. So we had this huge, brand spanking new, governmental, high-tech facility that provided the perfect shell for the secret base. We got to build exactly what we wanted inside—the isolation chamber, for example.

Barba: I assume the boat impound dock was in Seattle, too.

Roach: Yes, it's actually a maritime training academy. And that boat we used as the *Tarakan* is an ocean-going tug used for training purposes. But it was originally a drug-smuggling boat. It was involved in what is still the largest maritime narcotics bust in American history.

Barba: Wow. There were probably good ghosts in that boat providing atmosphere.

Roach: (laughs) Yeah, I think so. The boat was an ice-breaker with a huge metal plate along the hull. When the Coast Guard was trying to stop it, they were firing .60 caliber machine guns, and the bullets were just bouncing off the plate. I'm not sure how they finally managed to affect the arrest.

Agent Craig Willmore (Jordan Lee Williams) and Detective Mary Astadourian (Paige Witte) outside of the Gordon's Hauling office.

Barba: How did you create those melted blast effects on the hull?

Roach: The art direction on this whole project was just top-notch; I was really pleased with everything they did. But in creating the blast effects on the *Tarakan* façade we happened to use water-soluble paint. Of course, being in Seattle, it started to rain the day we began shooting there. And the first thing we realized was, "Oh God, the boat's running!" So every time we'd yell "Cut!" a dozen stagehands would run out with tarps so the melting effects wouldn't melt (laughs). Yeah, that was an interesting day.

Overall, the shoot was one of the coolest, most interesting, and most terrifying things I've ever done. For one thing, right off the bat we filmed with David Duchovny and Gillian Anderson. Because of some conflicts, we had to bump the Alaska secret base scenes up to the front of the schedule. So not only were we starting with David and Gillian, we were starting with David and Gillian in the secret base, by far the most complex sequence in terms of real time and all the different contingencies. Plus, the crew hadn't gotten to know one another yet. So we were all tossed right into the fire. Fortunately, it went well. And after that, the rest of the shoot seemed relatively easy.

Greg Roach directing
David Duchovny.

Barba: What was it like working with David Duchovny and Gillian Anderson?

Roach: I've worked with actors for the last 20 years and did quite a bit of it myself at one point in time (I was a member of the Screen Actors Guild for a while), so I understand actors and speak their language fairly well. When you run across world-class talent you know it immediately.

David and Gillian have both really grown into their roles, both on- and off-camera. When we first started this project (three years back), they were more or less unknown, but by the time we began filming they had become household names. At first we were pretty intimidated, but they're both professional, and we really enjoyed the opportunity, especially with Gillian.

I think Gillian is one of the finest actresses of her generation and it was a real rush to be able to work with talent like that. As a matter of fact, she had such a good time on our shoot that we wrote some extra scenes for her and brought her back for additional filming. As a performer there's so much that goes on behind her eyes—she infuses every moment with such life, it's just a joy to see.

May 21, 1998
Boulder, CO
Seattle, WA

The X-Files Chronology

The following synopses of episodes from the first six seasons of *The X-Files* were distilled from the in-depth case file summaries in *The X-Files Unrestricted Access*, the definitive interactive resource on *The X-Files*. Our thanks go to Fox Interactive and Twentieth Century Fox Film Corporation for permission to use this material.

Season One

PILOT 1X79

FBI Agent Dana Scully is reassigned to a new position as Agent Fox Mulder's partner in the X-Files section, devoted to the exploration of unexplained and possibly paranormal phenomena. Their first case together is an investigation of the mysterious deaths of several high school classmates in Bellefleur, Oregon.

DEEP THROAT 1X01

Acting on a tip from a mysterious source (Deep Throat), Mulder and Scully travel to Ellens Air Force Base in Idaho to investigate the unusual disappearance of a military test pilot. In the process, they observe unidentified, presumably military aircraft conducting spectacular maneuvers. Seth Green guest-stars as a spaced-out teenager.

SQUEEZE 1X02

Mulder and Scully try to track a "human enigma," a killer named Eugene Victor Tooms, who can elongate his body and gain access to seemingly inaccessible places. The agents learn that Tooms awakens from hibernation every 30 years to commit five murders that include the forced extraction and consumption of each victim's liver.

CONDUIT 1X03

A teenage girl, Ruby Morris, is kidnapped from a campground near Lake Okobogee, Iowa. The abduction appears to be the work of extraterrestrial forces, prompting Mulder to face his feelings about the similar disappearance of his own sister, Samantha, when he was 12. The agents discover that Ruby's brother, Kevin, is receiving odd transmissions via the family TV set.

THE JERSEY DEVIL 1X04

Scully and Mulder investigate the discovery of a mutilated human corpse thought to be the work of a legendary man-beast which, according to folklore, lives in the New Jersey woods. Known as the Jersey Devil, the creature has been terrorizing the southern part of the state for two centuries.

SHADOWS 1X05

The CIA requests the assistance of Agents Mulder and Scully in the

ICE 1X07

A team of researchers at an Icy Cape, Alaska research project is killed by an entity released when the team recovers a drilled ice core from the Arctic ice cap. Mulder and Scully and four companions investigate the deaths.

SPACE 1X08

An unknown force "possessing" a high-level NASA official is sabotaging the United States space shuttle program. Scully and Mulder must thwart the mysterious entity before the next shuttle launch.

FALLEN ANGEL 1X09

While investigating a meteor impact in Townsend, Wisconsin, Agent Mulder discovers what appears to be a UFO crash site. While detained by authorities, Mulder meets Max Fenig, another detainee captured near the site. The agents learn that Fenig appears to be an alien abductee.

EVE 1X10

Two identical murders involving "exsanguination" (extraction of all blood from the body) of the victims occur simultaneously in Greenwich, Connecticut and Marin County, California. Each killing involves a strange young girl, who happens to be one of a set of identical twins conceived in a secret government project gone awry.

FIRE 1X11

Mulder and Scully investigate an arsonist who apparently immolates his victims without leaving traces of accelerant or other incriminating elements at the crime scenes. They discover a man who can kill via pyrokinetics—using his mind to ignite fire.

BEYOND THE SEA 1X12

Agents Scully and Mulder seek the aid of Luther Lee Boggs, a notorious serial killer on death row, who claims to have psychic knowledge of the whereabouts of a pair of college students kidnapped in Raleigh, North Carolina.

GENDERBENDER 1X13

Agents Scully and Mulder focus on an isolationist religious order known as the Kindred (distinctive for abstinence and strong Christian values) as they investigate a bizarre series of murders along the Eastern Seaboard. The murders seem to have been committed by a single individual who kills as both a male and a female. This episode marks the first appearance of Nicholas Lea, though not as Alex Krycek. He plays one of the killer's near-victims.

LAZARUS 1X14

YOUNG AT HEART   1X15

A murderer, John Barnett, is supposed to have died in prison but returns in a new spree of robbery and homicide in Washington, D.C. One element of the spree is a series of notes taunting the FBI agent—Fox Mulder—who originally apprehended Barnett during an armored car heist.

E.B.E.   1X16

During an investigation of an anomalous occurrence in Tennessee, Scully and Mulder uncover evidence of a government effort to transport the wreckage and alien occupant of a UFO originally shot down in Iraq. This episode introduces Mulder's trio of informants known as the Lone Gunmen.

MIRACLE MAN   1X17

Agents Mulder and Scully investigate Samuel Hartley, a young faith healer in Tennessee who appears to use his powers to both heal and kill his congregation.

SHAPES   1X18

Mulder and Scully travel to a Montana Indian reservation to investigate a series of gruesome deaths beginning in 1946 that seem to be caused by a Manitou, an evil spirit capable of changing human beings into beasts.

DARKNESS FALLS   1X19

Reports of missing loggers bring Mulder and Scully to a remote Pacific Northwest forest, where the felling of a 500-year-old tree has unleashed a killer plague of mite-like insects which feed on the enzymes of living creatures.

TOOMS   1X20

Mulder trails Eugene Victor Tooms, the serial killer from the "Squeeze" episode who extracts and eats human livers, after the mutant is paroled from prison to a halfway house. This episode introduces AD Walter S. Skinner.

BORN AGAIN   1X21

A little girl seems to be inhabited by the spirit of a murdered policeman who uses her to wreak his revenge on his murderers.

ROLAND   1X22

Mulder and Scully investigate the murders of several aeronautical scientists at the Mahan Propulsion Lab in Colson, Washington. Both deaths seem linked to a mentally handicapped janitor named Roland Fuller. The agents discover Fuller may be controlled by a head frozen in a cryogenic state.

THE ERLENMEYER FLASK   1X23

Under the guidance of Mulder's high-level informant Deep Throat, Mulder and Scully investigate the appearance (and subsequent disappearance) of a man with super-human strength, green blood, and the ability to breathe underwater. The agents learn that secret government agencies have been testing alien DNA on humans with unexpected results, and now seek to eradicate evidence of such tests. Deep Throat is fatally shot by the Crew Cut Man in this episode.

Season Two

LITTLE GREEN MEN   2X01

With the X-Files shut down, Mulder learns from Senator Matheson that a NASA listening outpost at the Arecibo Observatory in Puerto Rico has intercepted a microwave signal from deep space. When Mulder journeys secretly to the suspected alien contact site, Scully tries to follow his trail.

THE HOST   2X02

Scully's autopsy of a victim murdered in the New Jersey sewer system reveals a white fluke-worm feeding in the corpse's abdominal cavity. Upon further investigation of the murder, Mulder discovers a hideous genetic mutation known as the Flukeman. (This episode also introduces X, a mysterious insider who tells Mulder, "You have a friend in the Bureau.")

BLOOD   2X03

An extraordinary number of multiple homicides in Pennsylvania bring Mulder to the scene. He finds that a number of residents of Franklin, a small farming community, suddenly turned violent, apparently prompted by digital readouts in various electronic devices—pagers, fax machines, cell phones—telling them to kill.

SLEEPLESS   2X04

Mulder and a new partner, Agent Alex Krycek, investigate a secret Vietnam-era sleep eradication program run by the Marine Corps that is having deadly hallucinatory effects on surviving participants. In the process of uncovering evidence of the program, Mulder and Scully find themselves pitted against a concerted government cover-up effort.

DUANE BARRY: PART 1 OF 2   2X05

Mulder is called in to help negotiate a hostage situation involving a man, Duane Barry, who claims to be a UFO abductee and a victim of alien experimentation. Barry is finally captured, but manages to escape and kidnap Agent Scully.

ASCENSION: PART 2 OF 2   2X06

Mulder traces Duane Barry to Skyland Mountain, Virginia in a desperate search for Scully. During the pursuit, Agent Krycek tries to undermine Mulder's efforts. Mulder finds Barry, but Scully is gone; Barry claims "they" have taken her. Krycek, actually an undercover operative working for the Cigarette-Smoking Man, eventually disappears as well. Assistant Director Skinner re-opens The X-Files. The abduction storyline in this episode was written to accomodate Gillian Anderson's impending maternity leave.

3   2X07

Mulder looks into a series of vampiresque murders in Hollywood identical to the killings of six other victims in Memphis and Portland. During the investigation, Mulder discovers a trio who engage in what they call "blood sports"— drinking blood. Mulder finds himself attracted to one of the women, who claims to be trying to escape the group.

ONE BREATH   2X08

Scully suddenly reappears, alive but in a critical and comatose condition, at Northeast Georgetown Medical Center. Mulder learns that she seems to be a victim of genetic engineering experiments, and he fights to save her life. His efforts bring him to a direct confrontation with the Cigarette-Smoking Man.

FIREWALKER   2X09

Mulder and Scully investigate the death of a scientist in Caltech's Firewalker Project, a study of Mt. Avalon, an active volcano in Washington. While investigating the incident at the project's remote site, the agents stumble upon a deadly, silicon-based spore parasite.

RED MUSEUM   2X10

When a number of teenagers disappear from Delta Glen, Wisconsin, then mysteriously reappear with "He/She is One" written on their backs, Mulder and Scully investigate the possibility of demonic possession and the involvement of a radical religious group, the Red Museum. The agents uncover secret experimentation with inoculations made of an alien substance, and re-encounter Deep Throat's assassin, known only as the Crew Cut Man.

EXCELSIUS DEI   2X11

A nurse at Excelsius Dei, a convalescent home in Massachusetts, claims to have been raped and beaten by a frail, elderly man in the form of an invisible entity. When the man is later choked to death by an unseen force, Mulder suspects the home is a center of paranormal activity.

AUBREY   2X12

Mulder and Scully investigate a string of slayings in Aubrey, Missouri, which mirror serial killings in the same town in 1942, more than 50 years earlier. Referred to as the "Slash Killer," the 1940's murderer carved the word "sister" on his victims' chests with a razor blade. Further investigation revealed the unsettling possibility that the original killer's memory and personality had been genetically transferred to a new killer.

IRRESISTIBLE   2X13

A psychotic necro-fetishist named Donnie Pfaster works in the funeral industry to collect "trophies" of hair and fingernails from female corpses. Soon he escalates his obsession to grave desecration and, eventually, to murdering his "collectibles" himself to satisfy his need. His spree culminates in the abduction of Agent Scully.

DIE HAND DIE VERLETZT   2X14

Mulder and Scully journey to the small town of Milford Haven, New Hampshire, to investigate the grisly, ritualistic slaying of a male teenager. The agents uncover a large Satanist cult, established in the area for more than three hundred years, and a mysterious woman with strange powers.

FRESH BONES   2X15

Mulder and Scully investigate the mysterious "suicides" of two Marine privates stationed at the Folkstone Processing Center in North Carolina, where more than 12,000 Haitians have been detained in a refugee camp. The agents find themselves caught in a secret war between the brutal camp commander, Col. Jacob Wharton, and a Haitian voodoo priest.

COLONY: PART 1 OF 2   2X16

Mulder and Scully investigate the deaths of three abortion clinic doctors in separate arson fires. When Mulder discovers that all three doctors looked identical, the agents' investigation leads to a shape-changing alien bounty hunter who is systematically terminating the cloned members of an alien hybrid colony established in the U.S. during the 1940s. This assassin abducts Scully in his search for the remaining colonists.

END GAME: PART 2 OF 2   2X17

The alien bounty hunter offers to trade Scully for Mulder's sister Samantha, who has returned 22 years after her abduction. After the exchange goes awry, Mulder learns that his "sister" may not be who she seems. His search ends in a dramatic confrontation with the assassin in the Arctic.

FEARFUL SYMMETRY   2X18

Mulder and Scully turn up evidence of animal abductions from the Fairfield Zoo in Idaho, near Mountain Home Air Base, a noted UFO "hotspot." Are these animals the beneficiaries of a radical animal rights group called the Wild Again Organization? Or are they targets of alien experimentation? Mulder finds answers from an unusual source: Sophie, a gorilla who can communicate via American Sign Language.

DOD KALM   2X19

A mysterious corrosive agent in the Norwegian Sea causes the crew of the navy destroyer U.S.S. Ardent to rapidly age and die. When Mulder and Scully investigate, they discover that the corrosion also affects the ship's hull, and they fall victim themselves.

HUMBUG   2X20

Mulder and Scully investigate the latest bizarre death in a string of homicides spanning 28 years. The killing occurs in a Florida town, home to many circus and sideshow performers, both retired and still employed. This episode features members of the Jim Rose Circus.

THE CALUSARI   2X21

A two-year-old boy's unusual death at a Virginia amusement park leads Mulder and Scully to the boy's brother, who seems to be inhabited by an evil presence. Their investigation leads them to a group of Romanian elders known as the Calusari, responsible for the correct observance of sacred rites.

F. EMASCULATA   2X22

When a deadly plague kills 10 prisoners inside the Cumberland Prison, Scully is called to the quarantine area while Mulder tracks two escapees who may also be infected. The agents uncover evidence of a covert bio-medical project gone awry; a killer parasite discovered by a research entomologist in the Costa Rican rain forest and carried by the F. Emasculata insect infected the inmates.

SOFT LIGHT   2X23

Mulder and Scully investigate a series of odd disappearances in Virginia, where the only trace of the missing victims is a scorch mark on the floor. The investigation leads them to a research company, Polarity Magnetics, where an accident during an experiment in particle astrophysics has turned a scientist's shadow into a kind of black hole, reducing all contacted matter into pure energy.

OUR TOWN 2X24

When a federal poultry inspector disappears in Arkansas, Mulder and Scully uncover murders and other strange secrets linked to the local chicken processing plant.

ANASAZI: PART 1 OF 3 2X25

An associate of the Lone Gunmen hacks into Defense Department computer systems and retrieves documents providing evidence of UFOs. Shortly after handing over a digital tape (encoded in Navajo) with the evidence to Agent Mulder, the man is killed. Mulder's father asks Mulder to travel to Martha's Vineyard so he can explain some things to his son. But before he can, Krycek fatally shoots him. Soon Mulder finds his own life in jeopardy, as well as the lives of other people close to him.

Season Three

THE BLESSING WAY: PART 2 OF 3 3X01

With the Cigarette-Smoking Man in hot pursuit of a digital tape that proves the existence of alien contact, Agent Scully finds herself suspended from her job and discovers a strange metallic implant in her neck. Meanwhile, a near-dead Mulder is nursed back to health in a Navajo ceremony.

PAPER CLIP: PART 3 OF 3 3X02

The agents learn they're targeted for death when Scully's sister Melissa is mistakenly shot by assassins seeking Scully. With Mulder, she goes underground to seek evidence of alien experimentation by Nazi war criminals who were allowed to escape to America after World War II— an exchange dubbed Operation Paper Clip. Meanwhile, Skinner tries to bargain with the Cigarette-Smoking Man for his agents' lives.

D. P. O. 3X03

Mulder and Scully travel to Connerville, Oklahoma to investigate a series of deaths attributed to lightning strikes. There, they find a teenage boy who can generate electricity and seemingly control lightning.

CLYDE BRUCKMAN'S FINAL REPOSE 3X04

Mulder and Scully join an investigation into a series of brutal murders of fortune-tellers in St. Paul, Minnesota. In searching for the killer, they meet an insurance salesman named Clyde Bruckman (Peter Boyle) with the ability to foresee how other people will die.

THE LIST 3X05

Before a death row inmate, Napolean "Neech" Manley, is executed in Florida, he vows to return from the dead and kill five people against whom he holds grudges. Mulder and Scully are called in after the dead man appears to be making good on his promise. J.T. Walsh guest-stars as Warden Brodeur.

2SHY 3X06

Mulder and Scully track a serial killer who meets overweight women via Internet chat rooms, then kills them and feeds on their body fats by secreting a viscous hydrochloric acid on the victims.

THE WALK 3X07

Mulder and Scully encounter a quadruple amputee veteran of the Gulf War who exhibits the power of astral projection as he terrorizes his former superiors and their families at Fort Evanston, Maryland.

OUBLIETTE 3X08

The kidnapping of a 15-year-old girl in Washington is physically experienced by a woman abducted by the same man years earlier. Mulder and Scully use the woman's feelings to trace the kidnapper.

NISEI: PART 1 OF 2 3X09

Video of an alien autopsy puts Mulder and Scully on the trail of a conspiracy involving an elite Japanese medical corps (Unit 731) known to have experimented on human subjects during World War II. The investigation introduces Scully to members of MUFON, a network of victims of alien abduction and experimentation, casting light on Scully's own abduction.

731: PART 2 OF 2 3X10

Mulder believes a Japanese medical team has been developing an alien-human hybrid in a secret government network of rail cars. In pursuing this theory, he gets trapped aboard a train with an NSA assassin. Meanwhile, Scully learns disturbing new information about her neck implant, a sophisticated device with the ability to record certain brain functions.

REVELATIONS 3X11

When a delusional killer murders eleven stigmatics (individuals exhibiting wounds paralleling the Passion of Christ), Mulder and Scully seek to protect a young boy in Loveland, Ohio, who also displays the bleeding wounds. The assignment spurs Scully to question her own faith.

WAR OF THE COPROPHAGES 3X12

In Miller's Grove, Massachusetts, deaths apparently caused by an infestation of mutant killer cockroaches cause widespread panic. Mulder and Scully's investigation leads them to a waste research facility … and the possibility that the cockroaches are mechanical extraterrestrial explorers.

SYZYGY 3X13

A rare alignment of planets on January 12, 1996 triggers strange behavior in all the townspeople of Comity, New Hampshire. In particular, two high school girls born on the same day seem driven by the "syzygy" to violent and inexplicable acts.

GROTESQUE 3X14

A serial slasher claims that a malevolent gargoyle-like spirit is responsible for the murders he commits. After his arrest, the murders persist. Mulder and Scully must work with a famed FBI behavioral scientist, whose strained history with Mulder clouds the investigation.

PIPER MARU: PART 1 OF 2 3X15

A French salvage ship, the Piper Maru (named for Gillian Anderson's daughter), finds the mysterious wreckage of a World War II fighter plane, a P-51 Mustang. But the crew's exploration unleashes apowerful, oil-based alien entity capable of inhabiting human hosts and emitting deadly radioactive energy. The episode culminates with the shooting of Assistant Director Skinner.

APOCRYPHA: PART 2 OF 2 3X16

Mulder pursues the traitorous (and alien-inhabited) Krycek and the mystery of the sunken World War II wreckage, while DNA evidence from the assassination attempt on Skinner links the assassin, Luis Cardinal, to the murder of Scully's sister. Mulder learns that the alien uses common diesel oil as a medium for "body-jumping" from host to host.

PUSHER 3X17

Mulder and Scully investigate a contract hit man who murders using psychokinetic power to will people to commit suicide. Known as the Pusher, the suspect engages Mulder in a deadly battle of wills.

TESO DOS BICHOS 3X18

The removal to a Boston museum of skeletal remains from the Teso dos Bichos Excavation Project in the Ecuadorian jungle results in a series of deaths potentially linked to a feline shaman spirit.

HELL MONEY 3X19

The crematorium deaths of eleven Chinese immigrants whose bodies exhibit signs of pre-mortem removal of multiple organs leads Mulder and Scully to a macabre lottery-style game with potentially fatal consequences.

JOSE CHUNG'S FROM OUTER SPACE 3X20

An author of "non-fiction science fiction" interviews Agent Scully about the rumored UFO abduction of two teenagers in Klass County, Washington that seems open to a number of wildly variant interpretations. Scully writes it off as a case of date rape until a pair of AWOL Air Force pilots turns up dead under mysterious circumstances.

AVATAR 3X21

Skinner awakens in a hotel room with a dead woman whose neck has been violently twisted. Was he framed? Mulder and Scully learn that Skinner has sought treatment for a sleep disorder, citing a recurring "night terror" in which the specter of an old woman tries to suffocate him.

QUAGMIRE 3X22

Mulder and Scully investigate a series of gruesome deaths (including that of Scully's dog, Queequeg) around Heuvelmans Lake in Georgia that may be the work of a lake monster known locally as Big Blue.

WETWIRED 3X23

An informant alerts Mulder and Scully to a secret government conspiracy involving subliminal mind control through television signals that trigger the deep fears of exposed subjects. When the experiment induces a series of murders in a small Maryland town, the agents investigate, and Scully herself becomes afflicted.

TALITHA CUMI: PART 1 OF 2 3X24

Two events—the miraculous recovery of four gunshot victims in a Virginia fast-food restaurant, and a sudden stroke suffered by Mulder's mother—send Mulder and Scully in search of a mysterious man, Jeremiah Smith, who has the power to heal. But Smith's existence is linked to a conspiracy involving the alien colonization of Earth, and he is a target of the same alien bounty hunter seen earlier in "Colony" and "End Game."

Season Four

HERRENVOLK: PART 2 OF 2 4X01

As Mulder's mother lies dying, Jeremiah Smith leads him to a farm compound of mute children; Mulder is stunned to discover that all of the girls are clones of his long-missing sister, Samantha. Meanwhile, Scully's research offers glimpses of a plan to use smallpox scars to secretly catalog all inoculated human beings. X is assassinated, but leaves a cryptic message for Mulder in his own blood, leading Mulder to a new "inside" source of information.

THE X-FILES: AGRIPPA 3X99

In the timeline, this is when the events in the game take place.

UNRUHE 4X02

A murder-kidnapping in Traverse City, Michigan, puts Mulder and Scully on the trail of a twisted killer who abducts young women and performs transorbital lobotomies before releasing them. A series of photos depicting the killer's sick fantasies seem to be an example of "psychic photography."

HOME 4X03

While investigating the death of a horrifically deformed infant found buried in the small rural community of Home, Pennsylvania, Mulder and Scully discover a family of men afflicted with numerous disfiguring congenital defects resulting from generations of inbreeding. (This episode features a local sheriff named Andy Taylor with a deputy named Barney.)

TELIKO 4X04

African-American men are disappearing. Their bodies, when found, are completely drained of pigment. At first, Scully suspects they were killed by a virulent new disease. But the investigation leads to an African immigrant who lacks a pituitary gland and thus needs a steady supply of pituitary hormones from victims.

THE FIELD WHERE I DIED 4X05

Mulder and Scully investigate possible child abuse in the Temple of the Seven Stars, a religious cult based in Tennessee. The agents interrogate one of the polygamous cult leader's wives, Melissa Riedel, who seems to suffer from multiple personality disorder. But under hypnosis, she reveals accounts of past lives—including one of a Southern nurse who knew Mulder in 1863 as Sullivan Biddle, a Confederate soldier.

SANGUINARIUM 4X06

Cosmetic surgeons at Greenwood Memorial Hospital in Chicago suddenly begin murdering patients with the tools of their trade. Mulder and Scully uncover disturbing evidence pointing toward blood sacrifice and the practice of the black arts.

MUSINGS OF A CIGARETTE-SMOKING MAN 4X07

One of the Lone Gunmen, Frohike, claims to have uncovered the history of the Cigarette-Smoking Man, who listens from a sniper perch across the street. The tale of the man's life winds through just about every major conspiracy theory of the past 40 years. Chris Owens (later Special Agent Jeffrey Spender) guest-stars as the young cigarette-smoking man.

PAPER HEARTS 4X08

A disturbing dream leads Mulder to the burial site of a young girl murdered by a serial killer, John Lee Roche, who cuts hearts from the clothing of his victims. The murderer, already imprisoned after confessing to 13 other slayings, also claims to have been the abductor of Samantha Mulder.

TUNGUSKA: PART 1 OF 2 4X09

Mulder and Scully intercept a diplomatic courier bringing a chunk of meteorite containing a lethal alien life form—a single-celled organism that attacks and colonizes the body—into the United States. Further investigation points to a vast, high-level international conspiracy, taking Mulder to a remote Russian gulag in Tunguska, Siberia where unspeakable experiments are conducted.

TERMA: PART 2 OF 2 4X10

Imprisoned in the Tunguska gulag, Mulder is exposed to the alien biotoxin as part of a Russian experiment to find a cure for the "black cancer." Meanwhile, in Washington D. C., Scully learns more about the alien organism and faces a hostile Senate subcommittee investigation. The agents learn that the Cold War is not over.

EL MUNDO GIRA 4X11

A 19-year-old female migrant laborer is killed in the San Joaquin Valley of California by a strange yellow rain. Mulder and Scully discover another migrant worker who may be a carrier of an unknown enzyme, possibly extraterrestrial in origin, which stimulates massive fungal infections.

KADDISH   4X12

Members of an anti-Semitic gang are dying in mysterious ways. To find the truth, Mulder and Scully must explore the deepest secrets of Jewish mythology.

NEVER AGAIN   4X13

After reluctantly accepting an assignment out of town, a despondent Scully meets a single guy who seems to be having problems with his new tattoo (voiced by Jodie Foster). This is the first episode which aired out of order—filmed before, but aired after "Leonard Betts" (see following entry).

LEONARD BETTS   4X14

The corpse of a man decapitated in a car accident disappears from a hospital morgue. Mulder and Scully discover that the man, Leonard Betts, is able to regenerate cells rapidly to grow back lost body parts—even a head. In order to do this, however, he must feed on cancer. When Betts attacks Scully looking for "something he needs," she faces a blunt realization.

MEMENTO MORI   4X15

Scully learns she has inoperable cancer—the same type, a nasopharyngeal tumor, that killed a group of female UFO abductees. While she undergoes radical treatment, Mulder works with the Lone Gunmen to infiltrate the inner workings of the conspiracy behind her disease.

UNREQUITED   4X16

The murder of a Marine Corps general brings Mulder and Scully to Fort Evanston, Maryland, to investigate. They uncover ties to a radical paramilitary group, the Right Hand, which claims to have liberated a POW abandoned in Vietnam by his superiors. The prisoner, a former member of an elite Green Beret detachment, has returned to the United States to seek revenge, eluding detection by using a special talent for manipulating the sight of others.

TEMPUS FUGIT: PART 1 OF 2   4X17

Flight 549, an airliner carrying 134 people, crashes into the woods near Albany, New York, killing all passengers including the former UFO abductee, Max Fenig. Mulder suspects a conspiracy to kill Fenig, who claimed to be carrying a package containing physical proof of the existence of extraterrestrial life. He also suspects that a massive cover-up is underway, a belief verified by a military air traffic controller who witnessed the incident.

MAX: PART 2 OF 2   4X18

As Mulder seeks evidence of alien and government involvement in the crash of Flight 549, he finds a second crash site in nearby Great Sacandaga Lake. His discovery triggers a massive military disinformation campaign—and the deaths of several friends and colleagues, including Agent Pendrell.

SYNCHRONY   4X19

Time travel may be the key to solving several baffling murders on the campus of the Massachusetts Institute of Technology.

SMALL POTATOES   4X20

Mulder and Scully investigate several bizarre births in a small Southern town.

ZERO SUM   4X21

Skinner makes a deal with the Cigarette-Smoking Man to prevent Scully from dying of cancer.

ELEGY   4X22

Several young college-age women have been murdered in a single six-block area of Washington, D. C. Their prime suspect is a mentally disabled man, Harold Spüller, who has been beset by a series of frightening apparitions.

DEMONS   4X23

After experiencing a series of blackouts and seizures, Mulder believes he may be gaining new insights into Samantha's abduction. However, while taking his inner journey, he may also have unknowingly killed two people.

GETHSEMANE: PART 1 OF 3   4X24

When a Smithsonian forensic anthropologist claims to have discovered the 200-year-old body of an E.B.E. (extraterrestrial biological entity) frozen in ice in the Yukon Territory, Mulder and Scully pursue the story. What they find is shocking: An assertion that their work in The X-Files is merely part of a complex scheme to promote false beliefs in alien life, diverting attention from the dubious practices of the U. S. military.

Season Five

REDUX: PART 2 OF 3   5X02

Scully and Mulder engineer Mulder's "death" to create a cover for their investigations. Mulder uses the cover to infiltrate a secret research facility. Is it a center for DNA testing or a repository for extraterrestrial materials? In either case, it may hold a cure for Scully's alien cancer, as well.

REDUX II: PART 3 OF 3   5X03

Mulder's continuing search for a cure to Scully's cancer also puts him on the trail of a mole within the FBI. Is it Skinner? Some think so. The Cigarette-Smoking Man arranges a meeting between Mulder and a woman claiming to be Samantha, and makes several other appearances, too—plus a somewhat dramatic disappearance.

UNUSUAL SUSPECTS   5X01

This flashback episode depicts the original meeting of the Lone Gunmen—Langly, Byers, and Frohike—at (where else?) a computer show in a convention center. The three cyber-geeks try to assist a woman who claims knowledge of a secret government experiment using paranoia-inducing gas on human guinea pigs.

DETOUR   5X04

When people begin disappearing in a remote region of North Florida, Agents Mulder and Scully investigate the possibility that primitive humanoid predators are prowling the area.

CHRISTMAS CAROL: PART 1 OF 2 5X05

Scully joins her family in San Diego for the holidays. But a chilling phone call from an apparent suicide victim leads Scully to the home of a young girl whose resemblance to Scully's dead sister, Melissa, is haunting. When preliminary tests suggest the girl indeed may be Melissa's daughter, Scully pursues further DNA testing … which provides shocking results.

EMILY: PART 2 OF 2   5X07

After Scully learns she is the biological mother of Emily Sims, the agents slowly uncover a murky conspiracy surrounding the girl. It seems she is the subject of a ghoulish genetic experiment that began with Scully's abduction and is culminating in the cross-breeding of human and alien life forms.

THE POST-MODERN PROMETHEUS   5X06

Agents Mulder and Scully investigate a rural Indiana neighborhood in search of a monstrous, Frankenstein-like creature (dubbed "The Great Mutato") with a penchant for singer/actress Cher and peanut butter sandwiches.

KITSUNEGARI   5X08

The infamous Robert Modell (AKA "Pusher" from episode 3X17) escapes from prison, leading Agents Mulder and Scully on a chase that uncovers Modell's dangerous new ally.

SCHIZOGENY   5X09

A teenaged boy in Coats Grove, Michigan, apparently murders his abusive stepfather. But Mulder and Scully's investigation leads to a deeper mystery with answers that lie deep within the dark orchards that surround the town.

CHINGA   5X10

Residents of Amma Beach, Maine, are convinced that witchcraft is behind a recent spate of odd, self-mutilating "suicides." Agent Scully, vacationing in the town, discovers a frightening connection to a young girl's doll, Chinga. This episode was written by Chris Carter and Stephen King.

KILL SWITCH   5X11

A sentient artificial Internet intelligence evolves into a super-intelligent and dangerous entity that turns on its creators with a deadly vengeance. Mulder and Scully learn that only a special virus program dubbed "Kill Switch" can eliminate the rogue system. This episode was written by William Gibson and Tom Maddox.

BAD BLOOD   5X12

Mulder and Scully each recount their own version of the events that lead to Mulder's killing of a young man believed to be a vampire. Luke Wilson guest-starts as Sheriff Hartwell.

PATIENT X: PART 1 OF 2   5X13

Groups of UFO abductees gather first in Kazakhstan, then at Skyland Mountain, only to be burned alive by faceless assailants. In a role reversal, a skeptical Mulder (who sees a government bio-chemical weapons experiment gone awry) and a believing Scully investigate the gruesome mass burnings. Meanwhile, events reveal the shadowy outlines of a conflict pitting alien colonists (and their human allies in the Syndicate) against mysterious alien enemies. This episode introduces Special Agent Jeffrey Spender.

THE RED AND THE BLACK: PART 2 OF 2   5X14

Scully survives another mass burning of UFO abductees at Ruskin Dam, then undergoes hypnosis in an effort to remember what happened at the site. Meanwhile, the conflict between alien colonists and resistance fighters finally comes to light, and a possible vaccine against the alien black oil virus is recovered. An old nemesis reappears as well, claiming to be Agent Spender's father.

TRAVELERS   5X15

Grisly murders in 1952 seem linked to Mulder's father and Roy Cohn, infamous counsel to Sen. Joseph McCarthy during the HUAC "Red Scare" hearings of that era. X-philes will notice that a young Mulder is shown smoking and wearing a wedding ring. Hmmm ... .

MIND'S EYE   5X16

Agent Mulder believes a blind woman can see through the eyes of a murderer. Or is it a ploy to cover up her own murderous behavior? Lily Taylor was nominated for an Emmy for her guest appearance as Marty Glenn.

ALL SOULS   5X17

When a wheelchair-bound girl suffering from severe retardation and spinal deformities suddenly walks into a thunderstorm and dies a mysterious death, her priest asks for Scully's help in solving the case.

THE PINE BLUFF VARIANT   5X18

A terrorist militia group possesses a killer bioweapon that can eat living flesh. Mulder goes deep undercover to infiltrate the group. Is it a Russian-developed toxin, or is the U.S. government responsible for the deadly pathogen? And how is it being spread?

FOLIE À DEUX   5X19

A man named Gary Lambert believes his boss is an evil monster who preys on his own staff, turning them into zombie minions. When Mulder is sent to investigate, Gary takes him hostage.

THE END   5X20

A young boy named Gibson Praise exhibits remarkable clairvoyant powers ... and is targeted for elimination by the Syndicate. Tests on the boy reveal a massively developed region of his brain that may provide proof of a genetic link to an alien race. Meanwhile, Mulder and ex-flame Special Agent Diana Fowley renew their "chemistry," a bond unhappily noted by Scully. Mimi Rogers plays Fowley.

Season Six

FIGHT THE FUTURE

In this feature-length movie spanning Seasons Five and Six, Mulder and Scully finally uncover the enormity of the conspiracy between the Syndicate and the alien colonization effort. The agents discover a massive plan to infect and eliminate mankind using specially bred bees and corn. When Scully is abducted and becomes a doomed "host" at an alien breeding facility, Mulder must infiltrate the place and try to save her. Martin Landau co-stars as Dr. Alvin Kurtzweil.

THE BEGINNING   6X01

Mulder and Scully must find hard scientific proof of extraterrestrial life to justify the continued existence of the X-Files. To do so, Mulder tracks a deadly creature in the Arizona desert, while Scully runs medical tests on Gibson Praise, the young boy with alien powers. In this episode, Mulder and Scully are given a new boss—A.D. Kersh.

DRIVE   6X02

Mulder is kidnapped in the Nevada desert by Patrick Crump, a man who appears deranged with head pain. Scully, however, learns that external forces may be the cause of Crump's pain.

TRIANGLE   6X03

Agent Mulder's trip to the infamous Bermuda Triangle lands him aboard a ship lost at sea in 1930. Soon he learns he's in a time warp and has the ability to change history … for the worse. This episode was inspired by the classic Alfred Hitchcock film *Rope*.

DREAMLAND: PART 1 OF 2   6X04

Mulder and Scully finally stumble upon the motherlode of UFO lore—Area 51 in Nevada. But then a mysterious heat ripple emitted from a UFO switches the personalities of Agent Mulder and an Area 51 official named Morris (played by Michael McKean). Can Mulder convince a skeptical Scully of his plight?

DREAMLAND II: PART 2 OF 2   6X05

Mulder, imprisoned in the body of Morris, tries to escape Area 51 and resume his normal life. Meanwhile, Scully finally begins to suspect that her Mulder-looking partner is not really Mulder. (For one thing, he's tidy!) When Morris admits he's not Mulder, Scully searches for a way to re-swap their personalities.

TERMS OF ENDEARMENT   6X06

Scully accuses a woman of self-aborting her deformed fetus, but Mulder suspects more demonic forces at work. Bruce Campbell guest-stars as Wayne Weinsider.

THE RAIN KING   6X07

A brutal nine-month drought in Kroner, Kansas brings Mulder and Scully to the stricken town. The local sheriff believes a man has actually caused the drought to profit from selling rain. But the agents discover another possible cause for the odd weather phenomena. Victoria Jackson guest-stars as Sheila Fontaine.

HOW THE GHOSTS STOLE CHRISTMAS   6X08

On Christmas Eve, Mulder lures Scully into the stakeout of a reputed haunted house, where the ghosts of two star-crossed lovers (played by Ed Asner and Lily Tomlin) convince the agents to perform dangerous acts.

TITHONUS   6X09

Assistant Director Kersh assigns Scully a new partner, Peyton Ritter. Together they investigate a New York City case in which a crime-scene photographer may be committing the murders he documents for police.

S. R. 819   6X10

Apparently, someone has poisoned Assistant Director Skinner; Agents Mulder and Scully have 24 hours to find out who and why. But the truth may be more complex than a simple poisoning attempt.

TWO FATHERS: PART 1 OF 2   6X11

Secret government medical operatives seem to have created their first successful human/alien hybrid—none other than Cassandra Spender, Agent Spender's mother. But a unit of faceless alien rebels incinerates the medical team, bringing Mulder and Scully to the scene. Cassandra, who escaped the attack, tells the agents two disturbing things: the successful hybrid experiment will trigger alien colonization, and the colonists plan to use the black oil virus to wipe out all other life forms in the known universe.

ONE SON: PART 2 OF 2   6X12

Mulder finally learns the truth of the government/alien conspiracy while holding the Cigarette-Smoking Man at gunpoint—including the role his own father and sister played in the murky plot. Meanwhile, Scully suspects Agent Fowley of Syndicate connections, and Spender discovers that the final exchange between the Syndicate and the alien colonists is in motion. Spender meets his unfortunate end in this episode.

ARCADIA   6X13

Strange disappearances in a suburban planned community bring Mulder and Scully, posing as a married couple, onto the scene. In the process the agents unearth some bizarre and ancient Tibetan secrets.

AGUA MALA   6X14

While stranded in Florida by a hurricane, Mulder and Scully take refuge against the storm in an old apartment building. There the agents discover something terrifying in the water.

MONDAY   6X15

A blue Monday goes from bad to worse for Mulder and Scully when both get caught in the same desperate bank robbery again and again and again. Only the robber's girlfriend holds the key to escaping from the tragic time cycle.

ALPHA   6X16

A series of vicious dog attacks leaves a trail of death that brings Agents Mulder and Scully to the case. They discover that the killer beast may not be purely canine, but a deadly shapeshifter.

TREVOR   6X17

Pinker Rawls, a convict in Mississippi, seems capable of moving through solid objects. After he escapes from prison, Mulder and Scully follow his trail of vengeance—and discover Rawls's power is electrical.

MILAGRO   6X18

Mulder's next-door neighbor, a writer named Padgett, becomes the primary suspect in a series of grisly murders in which the victims' hearts are removed with no incisions or forensic evidence of any kind. Mulder suspects "psychic surgery." Meanwhile, Scully grows oddly attracted to Padgett.

THREE OF A KIND   6X19

In an attempt to infiltrate a defense contractor convention in Las Vegas, the Lone Gunmen run into Susanne Modeski (from episode 5X01, "Unusual Suspects"), who now appears to be brainwashed, perhaps by the very "psych warfare" E-H gas she invented. But the situation grows more complex as others, including Scully and two card-carrying conspiracy geeks named Jimmy and Timmy arrive on the scene.

THE UNNATURAL   6X20

This episode, written and directed by David Duchovny, features a superstar black baseball player in Roswell, New Mexico, who happens to be an alien. His exploits attract the first attention of the alien bounty hunter. This episode aired the day David Duchovny's daughter was born.

FIELD TRIP 6X21

Two skeletons turn up in the Brown Mountain region of North Carolina, near a mysterious mountain that has exhibited strange lights for centuries. When Mulder and Scully investigate, they fall victim to an odd phenomenon that may be triggered by wild mushrooms in the area. Is it hallucination—or something far worse?

BIOGENESIS: PART 1 OF 3 6X22

Odd metallic objects found in Africa appear to provide proof that life on Earth originated elsewhere in the universe. As Agents Mulder and Scully pursue this theory, they uncover a secret code that seems to be an alien map to the genetic makeup of mankind. Could our progenitors truly be alien? As they seek the answer to this question, the agents run into unexpected stumbling blocks—Mulder is afflicted with psychosis, while Scully grows suspicious of Assistant Director Skinner and Agent Fowley's interest in the case.

Bibliography

Goldman, Jane. The X-Files *Book of the Unexplained, Volume I*. New York: HarperPrism, 1995.

Goldman, Jane. The X-Files *Book of the Unexplained, Volume II*. New York: HarperPrism, 1996.

Lowry, Brian. *The Truth Is Out There: The Official Guide to* The X-Files , *Volume 1*. New York: HarperPrism, 1995.

Lowry, Brian. *Trust No One: The Official Third Season Guide to* The X-Files, *Volume 2*. New York: HarperPrism, 1996.

Meisler, Andy. *I Want to Believe: The Official Guide to* The X-Files, *Volume 3*. New York: HarperPrism, 1998.

Meisler, Andy. *Resist or Serve: The Official Guide to* The X-Files, *Volume 4*. New York: HarperPrism, 1999.